COLLECTING
FURNITURE
The Facts At Your Fingertips

COLLECTING
FURNITURE
The Facts At Your Fingertips

CHRISTOPHER PAYNE

General Editor:
Janet Gleeson

Miller's Collecting Furniture
The Facts at Your Fingertips

First published in Great Britain in 1995
by Miller's, a division of Mitchell Beazley,
imprints of Octopus Publishing Group Ltd.

Revised edition 1998

This 2001 edition published by
Chancellor Press, an imprint of Bounty Books,
a division of Octopus Publishing Group Ltd,
2-4 Heron Quays, London E14 4JP

Executive Editor Alison Starling
Editor Francesca Collin
Executive Art Editor Vivienne Brar
Art Editor Prue Bucknall
Designer Louise Griffiths
Special Photography Ian Booth, Jacqui Hurst
Illustrations Elly King
Indexer Hilary Bird

A CIP catalogue record for this book is available from the
British Library

ISBN 0 7537 0491 9

Set in Bembo

Printed and bound by Toppan Printing Co., Hong Kong

Cover Pictures: An 18th-century mahogany dining chair, £150–200; a 19th-century library table, £200–300; a Rennie Mackintosh chair, c.1896–7, £80,000-100,000; a French 19th-century giltwood and ormolu *bombé* commode, £6,000-10,000. *picture pages 2 & 3:* a late George II washstand, c.1800, £250–350; a Victorian pine chest, c.1870, £250–300; a William IV mahogany bergère, c.1830, £2,000–2,500; a late George III dumb waiter, c.1800, £1,000–1,500; a Biedermeier satin-birch sofa, c.1800, £2,000–2,500; a Victorian papier-mâché chess table, c.1840, £500–800; a 1920s display cabinet, £500–800, a 1952 wire chair designed by Harry Bertoia, £300–400; a Victorian armchair, c.1895, £300–500; a George III serpentine mahogany chest, c.1770, £2,500-3,000; a George III shield-shaped dressing-mirror, c.1780, £200–300, a George III mahogany cellaret, c.1770, £2,500–3,500; a Charles I oak joint stool, c.1620, £2,000–2,500; a Victorian child's high chair, c.1860, £150–200.

CONTENTS

INTRODUCTION

My life in the world of antique furniture started almost from the womb. My father always had a passion for old English furniture, as did my grandfather, who started a little corner shop in 1900 selling modern items. During World War I he could not obtain the supplies he needed so he started to look for what he called 'second-hand furniture' (now catalogued as Queen Anne!). I dread to think of the price of a lovely walnut tallboy in 1900 – no more than a few guineas, and now, ten or twenty thousand pounds!

My personal interest started as soon as I passed my driving test, aged 17. During the school holidays I would drive my father around the country as he bought furniture. Without realizing it, I started to go in to see his clients and to pick up an interest in what has become a lifetime's passion and a career that has lasted for over 30 years.

The real learning curve started in 1970, when, for three months, I joined the auctioneers, Sotheby's, as a porter in order to learn the trade, so I thought. I carried everything from Chelsea teapots to Roman sarcophagi up and down rickety old stairs. As time went by, the clients (especially those from overseas) would ask my opinion. It is amazing what could and still can be learnt in the salerooms. Famous people and notables from all walks of life wandered through the galleries, from pop stars to conductors, from financiers to eastern potentates, all with their own tastes and experiences to share.

Above all, the dealers and die-hard collectors were always willing to share their extensive knowledge. They were an invaluable source of instruction and I am eternally grateful to them for their friendly generosity.

As with any business, the world of antique furniture has changed dramatically over the years, becoming increasingly international. As I have travelled the world in the hunt for antiques, natural disasters have come and gone. Over the years I have seen chandeliers swinging into each other during an earthquake in Los Angeles and watched as a Georgian table floated out of a house in an Australian flood. I saw container-loads of furniture go off to America in the 1970s and arranged for container-loads to come back to London for sale in the 1980s.

Unfortunately there are no shortcuts to becoming an expert in furniture. My first, unforgettable, commercial lesson was in 1973, when I was shown a set of five so-called Irish Chippendale chairs and valued them at £2,000–2,500 – more than a year's salary at the time. After some research, we discovered that they were American and sent them to Sotheby's, New York, where they subsequently sold for $207,000. Another single chair from the set sold for $275,000 seven years later. In a relatively short time, the price had increased five-fold – a good early lesson in expertise and investment.

Antiques dealers have their own particular ways of teaching their trade. I remember one who asked how much a young runner had paid for a chair. On receiving the reply '£5', the dealer gave him the money and proceeded to smash the chair to pieces – telling his young protégé never to buy such rubbish again!

The trouble is that today's rubbish appears to be tomorrow's collectables, but the lesson can be adapted to say 'buy the best that you can afford'. Quality will out, even in a recession.

While many books on antiques feature the most expensive examples available, the furniture that we have chosen for *Collecting Furniture: The Facts At Your Fingertips* is made up, for the most part, of pieces that in my grandfather's day would have cost a few pounds. These are pieces that can be found today and bought on a fairly modest budget.

Furniture is an enormous and fascinating field that covers a wide range of materials, styles and uses. In this book there are chapters focusing on all of the major types of affordably priced items, including chairs, tables, sideboards and dressers, as well as furniture designed for the kitchen, bedroom and garden.

We have also included a section on major 20th-century designers. Examples of their work can still be found for very reasonable prices and, who knows, they might turn out to be the Chippendales and Hepplewhites of tomorrow.

The better informed you are about the main buying factors – styles, materials and methods of construction – the more likely you are to make a wise purchase and the more you will enjoy the experience of looking at and buying furniture. This book aims to answer all the questions a collector could ask and is packed with advice on authenticating, dating and valuing. A wide range of pieces, from medieval to modern, is examined in detail, using a methodical approach to decide what each one is, whether it is genuine and if it is worth buying. This guide offers hundreds of clues to help you identify and date individual pieces of furniture; it also shows you how to recognize styles, how to avoid fakes and how to spot a bargain.

When you begin buying furniture, use all your senses and skill. When attending an auction, make sure that you view the sale thoroughly beforehand, ideally twice and on separate days. Make sure that the saleroom catalogue includes a measurement for the widest part of each chest of drawers – usually the bracket feet, which are also the lowest and least accessible part. The feet can often stand out several inches from the sides. Similarly, when you

are measuring the inside of a niche, be sure to allow for the skirting boards, which take up several inches of space.

Always talk to the saleroom expert or antiques dealer before you buy. The more you have the opportunity to talk to experienced people the more you learn – even picking up the jargon will give you a head start.

Another consideration to bear in mind when buying furniture is the size of pieces. In the furniture world, small is beautiful. For instance, a Sutherland table or a butler's tray could be used anywhere. As a consequence, such pieces, although invariably they are relatively expensive, hold their value well.

The more experienced you become, the better the understanding you will have of the market value of an item. The prices in this book should act as a guide to help you gain some idea of value since they are based on current auction house and dealer prices. Bear in mind, however, that prices are always variable because no two pieces of furniture are exactly alike; there will always be subtle differences in colour and condition, if not in style.

I hope that this book, as you read and learn from it, gives you the confidence to explore this fascinating subject further. If you do so, I can only hope that you derive as much enjoyment from it as I have over the years.

CHRISTOPHER PAYNE

The values given in this book for featured objects reflect the sort of prices you might expect to pay for similar pieces at an auction house or from a dealer. As there are so many variable factors involved in the pricing of antiques, the values should be used only as a general guide.

PERIODS & STYLES

Dates	British Monarch	British Period	French Period
1558–1603	Elizabeth I	Elizabethan	Renaissance
1603–1625	James I	Jacobean	
1625–1649	Charles I	Carolean	Louis XIII (1610–1643)
1649–1660	Commonwealth	Cromwellian	Louis XIV (1643–1715)
1660–1685	Charles II	Restoration	
1685–1688	James II		
1688–1694	William & Mary	William & Mary	
1694–1702	William III		
1702–1714	Anne	Queen Anne	
1714–1727	George I	Early Georgian	Régence (1715–1723)
1727–1760	George II		Louis XV (1723–1774)
1760–1811	George III	Georgian	Louis XVI (1774–1793) Directoire (1793–1799) Empire (1799–1815)
1812–1820	George III	Regency	Restauration (1815–1830)
1820–1830	George IV		Charles X (1820–1830)
1830–1837	William IV	William IV	Louis Philippe (1830–1848)
1837–1901	Victoria	Victorian	2nd Empire (1852–1870) 3rd Republic (1871–1940)
1901–1910	Edward VII	Edwardian	

German period	US period	Style	Principal woods
Renaissance (to c.1650)	Seventeenth Century/ Pilgrim (1640–1690)	Gothic	Oak period (to c.1700, but 1750s in the provinces)
		Baroque (c.1620–1700)	
Renaissance/Baroque (c.1650–1700)			Walnut period (c.1690–1735)
	William & Mary (1700–1730)		
Baroque (c.1700–30)	Queen Anne (1725–1755)	Rococo (c.1695–1760)	
Rococo (c.1730–60)	Chippendale (1755–1790)		Early mahogany period (c.1735–1770)
Neo-classicism (c.1750–1800)	Federal (1790–1815)	Neo-classical (c.1755–1805)	Late mahogany period (c.1770–1850)
		Empire (c.1799–1815)	Satinwood (1740–1800)
Empire (c.1800–1815)	Classical/Empire (1815–1840)		
Biedermeier (c.1815–48 and 1880–1920)	Restauration/ Pillar and Scroll (1830–1865)	Regency (c.1812–1830)	Rosewood (1810–1850)
Revivale (c.1830–1880)	Gothic/Elizabethan Revival (1830–1865)	Eclectic (c.1830–1880)	Walnut (1840–1860)
	Rococo Revival (1840–1870)		
	Renaissance/Neo-Grec/Egyptian Revival (1855–1885)		
Jugendstil (c.1880–1920)	Innovative/Patented/ Exotic/Victorian (1850–1900)	Arts & Crafts (c.1880–1900)	Rosewood (1880–1900)
			Satinwood (1880–1920)
	Design Reform/ Arts & Crafts/Architects (1875–1920)	Art Nouveau (c.1890–1920)	

PART 1

BUYING & SELLING

FURNITURE

ABOVE REGENCY ROSEWOOD SETTEE
COVERED IN 'OLD GOLD VELVET'. £3,000–4,000

LEFT INSIDE AN ANTIQUES SHOP.

STARTING A COLLECTION

Few of us actually collect furniture. In its strictest sense, collecting is forming a coherent and logical array summarizing a particular period. This is a somewhat unrealistic goal in the furniture world, unless you have just inherited an enormous and empty country house, together with the appropriate fortune – or have just won the National Lottery!

In reality, the true collector amasses the objects of his or her passion for the sheer joy of ownership. Indeed ownership itself can become a secondary factor to the excitement of buying furniture – this is the thrill of the kill.

When we think of the traditional English furniture collection, we often think of one formed by inheritance. However, even for those of us fortunate enough to inherit, the matter is not cut and dried – what is inherited is not necessarily what is desired. Great Aunt Agatha's huge pedestal sideboard, say, coveted when setting up home, becomes an embarrassment in later years.

Most of us start our collections on our own, more or less from scratch. We would

A magnificent collection of British mid-17th-century walnut furniture.

like to recreate the ambience of earlier times in modern surroundings – but how to begin? It is not necessary to collect one period exclusively; to fill the house with Georgian furniture just because you have inherited your aunt's Chippendale bureau would be cripplingly expensive. Often it can be fun to give each room a distinctive period look, but much depends on the period of the house itself. Most of us live in houses that were built only in the last one hundred years; these houses cannot accommodate more than a couple of pieces of Georgian furniture in a single room.

The problem is one of scale – not only do the length and width of a room need to be taken into account, but also the ceiling height. The lower ceilings of a modern house will lend themselves more easily to smaller pieces of Edwardian furniture.

Although the woods used in period furniture are distinctively different, they can be mixed in the same room. After all, that is what our ancestors did. Only the super rich would tear down a house and rebuild it to accommodate the newest fashions. A mixture of oak, mahogany and walnut of different styles and periods can often look very attractive.

By the same token, you should not ignore continental furniture. Many pieces are very elaborate and decorative, with fine marquetry, and make good focal points. Also, they can often be surprisingly cheap when not sold in their countries of origin.

When buying furniture for your house, visit all types of antiques shops and auction houses. Although there are many mysteries to discover about the antiques world, people are often reluctant to become involved in a purchase and to learn from it for the next time. Before you buy a piece of furniture, listen to all the contradictory opinions expressed about it. Above all, carefully examine what you are about to buy. A cursory glance is not enough: turn it over, examine it. Look at the colour of each leg – has one of them been replaced? Is the wear even? The more you look, the more you learn. Think of yourself as a detective and mentally take the piece apart bit by bit – it will help.

Patination is an all-important factor, especially on English pieces of furniture; English traditional taste appreciates the old, faded colour of antique furniture. One or two hundred years of dirt is the popular look – dealers prefer to buy pieces this way, even if they then repolish them for their customers. Generally speaking, pieces should be repolished only as a last resort, and then by a professional. French polish should always be avoided. It was popular in the early part of this century, a period when much good Georgian furniture was ruined.

Tastes vary around the world, however. Many pieces of English furniture, for example, were stripped and repolished to look bright and new before they were exported to countries such as Holland and Germany during the 1970s.

If pieces of veneer break off, do not throw them away; keep them safely, as it is always preferable to use original veneers, and they will reduce the cost of restoration.

Once you have chosen a particular style of furniture that suits your taste and your house, make sure that your home is a suitable environment for it. In the 18th century, damp was the main problem, while today heat and light are the enemies. Central heating dries the air and takes the moisture out of a piece of furniture, which means that the carcass can shrink, causing the veneers to crack.

Double-glazing a centrally-heated room will exacerbate the problem, allowing no

A pair of cabinets is always highly desirable. This walnut pair, made c.1840, are stamped by their makers, Wilkinson & Son, 8 Old Bond Street, London.

moisture into the room. With this in mind, an old-fashioned warehouse may prove to be the best place to store furniture over long periods – one with brick walls and a tiled roof, not a modern heat box. Wooden furniture slowly adapts its moisture content as the seasons gradually change; brick houses even out any dramatic change in the season. If a piece has been kept in an airy country house for the past 100 years, it may be as well to let it spend a few weeks in the garage rather than proudly exhibiting it in the sitting-room for Christmas. A humidifier will protect your investment – and your skin.

High-tech window film can be applied to glass to screen out the sun's damaging ultra-violet rays and to reduce heat and glare without distorting natural colour. Doing this can save your furniture from irreversible damage.

It gives great pleasure to sell at a profit after years of enjoying a piece of furniture. The pointers on the following pages of this book should help you to buy wisely. Remember, buy what you like and the chances are that someone else will like it too when the time comes to sell.

AUCTIONS

Hardly a day goes by without the national papers featuring a story about an amazing work of art that has been discovered and sold at auction for a fabulous sum of money. Although these news stories make fascinating reading, they tend to give buyers the misleading impression that only objects worth thousands of pounds are ever sold at auction.

Even the headline-hogging international auction houses sell far more modestly priced goods than expensive ones, and there is an enormous number of provincial auction houses holding regular furniture sales at which reasonably priced furniture is bought and sold.

Many new collectors are rather daunted by the prospect of visiting an auction house for the first time but, if you follow a few simple guidelines, buying furniture at auction can prove very affordable – and also great fun.

A sale of furniture at Sotheby's in London. Sotheby's, in common with all major auction houses, holds regular auctions of furniture throughout the year.

CATALOGUES

The items featured in an auction are listed in a catalogue in the order in which they are to be sold. The catalogue is usually published one or two weeks before the sale takes place. Depending on the auction house and the type of sale, catalogues range from a typed sheet to an elaborately illustrated glossy publication. If you intend to become a dedicated collector, you can subscribe to a series of catalogues from an auction house – invariably cheaper than buying them singly. Alternatively, you can telephone the saleroom and ask them to post you a copy of the catalogue, or buy one when you visit the viewing.

At larger salerooms the catalogue entry for each 'lot' (item in the sale) gives you a fairly detailed description of each piece of furniture, including the date it was made (although Christie's omits the date for modern items, so check the description carefully). The type of wood it is constructed from as well as any replacements or alterations are also noted. Many auction houses also offer a conditional guarantee of authenticity, so that if something described as '18th century' turns out to be a later copy you do have some recourse.

Most catalogues also include estimated prices. These give you an idea of what the auction house expects each piece to fetch at the sale, based on the prices realized by similar objects. The estimates are useful as general guides, but do not expect them to be one hundred per cent accurate. There are always some surprises, depending on the competition for a particular piece on the day; this is part of the thrill of buying at auction. Ultimately, any work of art, no matter how rare or valuable, is only worth at auction what two or more people are willing to pay for it, and this uncertainty gives auctions their special appeal.

VIEWING

A few days before a sale takes place, the furniture is put on view to the public. It is important to make the effort to view the auction properly beforehand. Do not expect to be able to view immediately prior to the auction, as the porters will often be rearranging the lots ready for sale. In any case, this is not usually a satisfactory time to examine furniture in detail – you might find someone comfortably seated, ready for the auction, on a chair that caught your eye in the catalogue. Remember that buying 'on spec' during a furniture auction is usually a rash move that you will regret.

When you view a furniture sale, make sure that you examine the pieces you are interested in carefully. Pull out drawers, look under table tops, lift chairs and look for indications of alteration, and check for signs of worm damage. If a cupboard or drawer is locked, you should not hesitate to ask a member of staff if it can be opened. Always try to look at the back of the piece as well as the front.

If you are uncertain about something, ask to speak to the expert in charge. He or she will probably be able to give you more information on the piece than was included in the catalogue description.

If the piece is damaged, take the cost of restoration into account before deciding on your bidding limit. Keep in mind that it is always worth considering several objects rather than setting your heart on just one. If the bidding goes beyond your limit on one piece, you can turn your attention to the next one.

> ### BUYING AT AUCTION CHECKLIST
> - STUDY THE CATALOGUE
> - REGISTER YOUR DETAILS BEFORE BIDDING
> - DECIDE ON YOUR LIMIT AND STICK TO IT

REGISTERING TO BID

Before you start bidding on the day of the sale, most auction houses expect you to register with their accounts department (giving your name and address, and possibly your bank details). Many salerooms issue you with a 'paddle number'. This is simply a card with a number on it that you show to the auctioneer should your bid be the successful one.

BUYING

When the sale begins, the auctioneer takes his seat on the rostrum and announces the lot number of the item to be sold. The object might then be held up at the front of the saleroom by the porters (or displayed on a closed-circuit television at grander establishments, such as Christie's and Sotheby's).

The bidding usually starts below the estimate and, depending on the value of the object, the price rises in increments of about 10 per cent of the estimated price.

An item that is estimated at £100–200, therefore, might rise in £10 increments, and a piece that is expected to realize £5,000–10,000 might increase by £500 a bid. However, it is important to bear in mind that the increments at each sale vary, and that they always do so entirely at the discretion of the auctioneer.

Many people bidding for the first time at auction are terrified at the prospect of coughing and landing themselves with a very expensive bill. In fact, this is almost impossible to do and in a packed saleroom you might find that you have to signal quite determinedly until you attract the auctioneer's attention for the first time. Once the auctioneer knows that you are interested he will glance back to you to see if you want to continue bidding. If you are the successful bidder, the auctioneer will knock the gavel down at the price reached. He will then ask you for your 'paddle number' and write this down in the 'auctioneer's book' as confirmation of the sale. You must remember that this act has the force of a legally binding contract, and you cannot change your mind after the gavel has fallen.

Many auctions contain hundreds of lots and last several hours. If you are interested in only one or two pieces at the end of the sale, you do not need to be present from the start of the auction. You can find out beforehand how quickly the sale is likely to proceed – the speed varies from about 60 lots per hour at major auctions, to over 120 in country sales. Save time by arriving shortly before the lot you want is offered.

A selection of furniture from a pre-sale viewing at Christie's South Kensington.

A regular weekly sale of furniture at Christie's South Kensington.

THE COST OF BIDDING

Bear in mind before you start bidding that on top of the hammer price (the price at which the bidding stops) you will have to pay the auction house premium, usually between 10 and 17 per cent, as well as VAT on the premium. If there is a dagger symbol or an asterisk by the catalogue description, then read the conditions of sale section of the catalogue; these symbols usually mean that VAT is to be added to both hammer price and premium.

ABSENTEE BIDS

If you are unable to attend the auction, you can leave a bid with the absentee bids office, and for no extra charge the commissions clerk or auctioneer will bid on your behalf. If you are undecided between two lots, you can leave 'either or' bids; in other words you can instruct the clerk to buy, say, lot 52 or, if unsuccessful, lot 75. Although the commissions clerk is bound to buy as cheaply as possible, it is always better to attend the sale in person.

PAYING AND COLLECTING

Make sure that you know the auction house's requirements for payment and collection before you buy. Most auction houses expect you to pay for and collect your furniture within a limited period of time (usually five working days). If you fail to do so, you will be charged interest on the outstanding amount and a storage fee. Many auction houses accept major credit cards, as well as cheques and cash.

If you buy an item that is too big to take

A black lacquer cabinet that sold for £1,250 at Christie's South Kensington.

home yourself, the auction house usually recommends a shipper. However, the buyer is responsible for any transportation costs.

SELLING AT AUCTION

There is usually no charge for an over-the-counter valuation for a piece of furniture at an auction house and you are not committed to sell afterwards if you do not want to. If the furniture you wish to sell is too large to transport easily, it is a very good idea to take some photographs of it. Send these to the auction house, along with the piece's dimensions, for an initial appraisal of the price it might fetch at auction.

Bear in mind that an auction house, unlike a dealer, does not buy your property from you, it sells it on your behalf. For this service you will probably be charged a commission of between 10 and 15 per cent of the hammer price. You will also pay VAT on the commission, an insurance charge and a handling charge. Christie's and Sotheby's have a sliding scale of charges, depending on the volume of goods you consign to them.

If your property is going to be illustrated in the auction catalogue you might be charged an additional fee to cover the costs of the photography. In the unlikely event of your property being unsold, there may be a buy back charge.

RESERVE PRICES

If the furniture you are selling is worth more than £500, the saleroom will probably advise you to put a reserve price on it. A reserve is the minimum price for which the auctioneer may sell your property so that if the auction should turn out to be poorly attended, your priceless property would not sell for £50. The reserve price is usually fixed at the bottom estimate or at between 10 and 15 per cent less.

ANTIQUES SHOPS & JUNK SHOPS

If you are an inexperienced collector and afraid of making expensive mistakes, buying from a reputable dealer is one of the safest ways to start collecting. But how do you go about finding a 'reputable' local dealer? One important thing to look for as you browse at the window of a tempting antiques shop is the logo of one of the leading antiques trade associations. If you buy antiques from a dealer who is a member of a recognized trade association you will be protected in several ways. In order to join the association the dealer will have had to demonstrate a sound knowledge of his or her subject. The stock in his or her shop will have been assessed to be of good quality, and he or she will have agreed to abide by a strict code of practice. A dealer who is a member of an association should display prices openly, describe stock accurately and treat customers fairly. Furthermore, in the unlikely event of any dispute over the authenticity of an object, the consumer has the bonus of a free conciliation service presided over by the association's committee.

In Britain, the largest associations are BADA (the British Antique Dealers' Association) and LAPADA (the London and Provincial Association of Art and Antiques Dealers). In the United States, the National Art & Antiques Dealers Association of America, Inc. and the Art & Antique Dealers League of America are similar bodies. There are also organizations in most European countries. If you contact one of these associations it will send you,

> **BUYING FROM A DEALER CHECKLIST**
> - PICK A REPUTABLE DEALER
> - COMPARE PRICES FOR SIMILAR PIECES SHOWN IN OTHER SHOPS
> - FIND OUT WHAT, IF ANY, RESTORATION HAS BEEN CARRIED OUT
> - TAKE YOUR TIME WHEN CHOOSING WHAT TO BUY
> - GET A DETAILED RECEIPT

free of charge, a list of its member dealers who specialize in furniture.

There are many advantages to buying from a dealer rather than at auction. First, you will not have to rush. There is no pressure to make up your mind in an instant as to how much you are willing to pay, which you may have to do in the heated atmosphere of the saleroom. You will also know exactly how much you are going to pay for the piece – there is no need to worry about adding VAT and the auction house premium onto the price quoted. You can take as long as you like (within reason) to make up your mind and some dealers will even let you take things on approval, clearly an advantage if you are worried about how a piece will look when you get it home.

Unlike auction houses, where furniture may be quite dilapidated, most quality dealers offer furniture in a good state of repair and will have the piece restored, if necessary, before offering it for sale. This means that there are no extra restoration costs to take into account.

If you get on well with your dealer, you might build up a long-lasting relationship that will be beneficial to both of you. Most dealers are great enthusiasts about their stock, they tend to buy to their own tastes and will probably be happy to share their knowledge of the subject as you build your collection. They might look out for special pieces that they do not have in

A general antiques shop in Brighton.

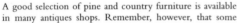

A good selection of pine and country furniture is available in many antiques shops. Remember, however, that some items will be modern reproductions. Look out for signs of genuine ageing, colour and condition.

stock for you or offer to buy back pieces they have sold to you, so that you can upgrade your collection.

BUYING FROM A DEALER

Once you have found a good dealer and spotted something in his shop that you want to buy, ask for as much information about the piece as possible. A good dealer will be glad to spend time talking to you, explaining the pros and cons of the pieces in which you are interested. The dealer should be able to tell you how old an item is, what it is made of, and from where it came (auction, private property or deceased estate). There may also be some interesting history or provenance to the piece. You should also ask what, if any, restoration has been carried out on the piece.

When it comes to agreeing the price there are no hard and fast rules, but in many antiques shops the first figure you are quoted is not the 'best' price and if you 'discuss' the sum you will often find that you can reduce it a little.

Once you have agreed to the price and paid for the piece, make sure that you are given a detailed receipt by the dealer, which should include:
● the dealer's name and address;
● the date;
● the price;
● a clear and accurate description of the item, including the approximate date that it was made.

Beware of descriptions that use the word 'style' and give no date of manufacture. A description that reads 'Queen Anne-style' and gives no date could mean that the piece was in fact made during the 20th century in the earlier style; whereas if it reads 'Queen Anne c.1702', it means that the piece was made c.1700 – in other words, during Queen Anne's reign.

SELLING TO A DEALER

The high profile of auction houses has meant that many people assume that they will get the best possible price by selling through an auction house, but this is not always the case, and it is always worth comparing the price a specialist dealer can offer you with the saleroom's valuation before you decide how to sell.

Before approaching a dealer, make sure that he specializes in the sort of piece you have to offer. There is no point asking a dealer in early English oak furniture if he wants to buy your Victorian *chaise longue*; offer it instead to a dealer who specializes in 19th-century furniture. If the piece is large and difficult to transport, it is a good idea to telephone the dealer beforehand to ask whether he might be interested in what you have to offer or to show him a photograph first. Then, if he is interested, he will probably be more than happy to come to see the piece.

Selling to a dealer has many advantages. The price you agree is the amount that you will receive – there are no hidden costs, such as the auction house premium, photographic charges, insurance and VAT, which would be taken from the hammer price if you sold at auction.

If you agree to sell a table to a dealer for, say, £500, you should receive a cheque for that amount almost immediately. If, on the other hand, your table fetches £500 in a saleroom, you will receive a cheque for £400.71 (based on a rate of 15 per cent commission, 1½ per cent insurance, £2 handling and VAT). If the piece appears in black and white in the sale catalogue, this could cost you a further £10–30.

You will also have to wait for a few weeks while your table is catalogued and entered in the appropriate sale. In many cases, you will not receive your cheque until several weeks after the sale. Bear in mind, too, that in the unlucky event of the piece not reaching its reserve at auction, this may make it more difficult to sell to the local trade.

In certain circumstances a dealer might agree to take a piece 'on consignment'. Be sure to obtain a signed contract from the dealer and to agree who is responsible for insurance. The contract should clearly state an agreed rate of commission.

JUNK SHOPS

There is a world of difference between an up-market dealer's showroom and a junk shop. Most junk shop owners find their stock from house clearances that will have been scoured by dealers first. Therefore, although you would be lucky to find a real 'treasure' in a junk shop, they are a great source of less expensive pieces of furniture (in particular 20th-century furniture). With a little care and attention, any such pieces can become just as attractive as more expensive antiques.

However, if you buy from a junk shop do not expect the same level of expertise that you would find at an established antiques dealer's outlet. Ask questions, but also make sure that you examine the piece as carefully as possible and make up your own mind as to its age, origins and authenticity. Also, always remember to take a torch as these shops sometimes have treasures tucked away in dark corners!

KNOCKERS

Never sell to people who turn up at your home uninvited or put notes through your door offering to buy unwanted antiques. Many of these so-called 'knockers' are highly disreputable and will try to trick you into parting with your property for much less than it is worth.

FAIRS & MARKETS

Antiques fairs have proliferated in recent years to become some of the most popular places to buy antiques. Each year various major and minor antiques fairs take place throughout Britain, continental Europe and the United States. Most dealers know the good sales potential of fairs and take stands at at a number of these antiques events.

LARGER FAIRS

If you are a fairly new collector of furniture, attending some of the larger antiques fairs is an interesting way to learn about furniture while you begin to accumulate a collection. As one of the most popular collecting fields, there will almost certainly be a variety of furniture dealers who are specialists in different types of furniture. Some stands may feature rustic oak or country furniture, other dealers may have

> **BUYING AT FAIRS & MARKETS CHECKLIST**
> - COMPARE PRICES AND STOCK AT SEVERAL STALLS
> - GET THERE EARLY TO FIND THE BEST BARGAINS
> - GET TO KNOW DIFFERENT DEALERS PERSONALLY
> - ASK FOR A WRITTEN RECEIPT FOR YOUR PURCHASE

classic 18th-century walnut and mahogany. Some may display nothing other than grand continental pieces, while others may have pieces in a variety of styles. There should certainly be no lack of choice!

Such a range, all under the same roof, gives you a chance to compare stock as well as prices. You will be able to decide what you like best, and who offers the best value, without using up too much of your shoe leather.

If you decide to visit one of the larger fairs, you will probably be charged an entry fee, for which you may also be given a list of the exhibitors, perhaps in a glossy catalogue. This list is a useful reference as it will include the stand numbers of exhibitors at the fair, as well as their business addresses and telephone numbers. Dealers use fairs as an important way of making contacts with potential new customers, as well as making sales, so they will usually be only too happy if you say that you will visit them after the fair. Bear in mind, however, that one result of the general recession of the past few years is that increasing numbers of dealers now operate from private residential addresses rather than shops, so find out if you need to telephone before you visit, in order to avoid disappointment.

VETTING

Larger fairs offer the added safeguard that all the exhibitors will have been carefully selected for their reputations and the quality of their stock, and each exhibit will have been 'vetted'. This means that each

This stand at the Kensington Antiques Fair has a good selection of pine and other country furniture.

piece will have been examined by a panel of independent experts (auction house valuers, museum curators and specialist dealers) to make sure that it is authentic and has not been over-restored. Some antiques fairs also have 'date-lines'; this means that anything exhibited must have been made before a specified date.

SMALLER FAIRS

As well as the large, grand fairs, numerous smaller antiques fairs take place throughout the country. At these, you will probably be charged an entrance fee, the goods may not have been vetted and the exhibitors may not have the same degree of expertise, but the goods offered will usually be less expensive. Fairs such as these can be great places to find 'bargains', but you do need to make up your own mind as to the age and authenticity of any piece you buy and to ensure that you get a proper receipt.

MARKETS

Antiques markets, in which you will find a concentration of furniture dealers with stands or shops, are another good place to buy furniture, especially if you arrive early enough to spot the best bargains before anyone else.

Some well-known antiques markets, such as Portobello Road in London, or the Flea Market (*Marché aux Puces*) in Paris, are so famous that they have become tourist attractions as well as the haunts of antiques collectors. Markets may take place on one or two days a week, or even every day (you can find out the times from the local tourist office).

Although some highly reputable dealers have stands and shops in markets, there are also less scrupulous dealers. The adage, *caveat emptor* (buyer beware), should always be kept in mind before you part with large amounts of money over a market stall where the dealer is not a member of a recognized trade association.

As when buying any antique, try to obtain a clearly written receipt for your purchase – one that includes the name and address of the dealer, with a description of the object and its approximate age. In this way, should you find out later that the object you have bought is not authentic, you will at least be covered by the laws of consumer protection.

Many people will remember the public outcry in Britain at the ancient laws of *marché ouvert* (open market), which until recently gave buyers of stolen property that had been purchased at some markets (such as the open areas of Bermondsey, London) the legal title to the goods.

Although this unpopular law has now been abolished, bear in mind that even after the change there is no guarantee that you will not be offered stolen property; if you buy it, you will simply have no title to it. Always choose your market stall with care before buying.

Dealers often arrange antiques into room settings.

OTHER SOURCES

Each year there are several well-publicized 'discoveries' that are bought at car boot sales and, after being identified as valuable works of art, resold for thousands of pounds. Stories such as these contribute greatly to the popularity of car boot sales, both with the general public and with dealers. Sometimes held in farmers' fields, school playgrounds or large car parks, they are advertised in many local newspapers, the classified columns of various magazines or on notices pinned to trees or lampposts in the area.

> ## BUYING AT A FLEA MARKET CHECKLIST
> - GET THERE EARLY
> - CARRY A TORCH
> - TAKE LOW VALUE NOTES IF YOU INTEND TO BUY
> - TRY TO GET A RECEIPT

Some boot sales are regular events held throughout the year, usually at weekends, while others are one-offs. You can sell anything at boot sales, and from the buyer's point of view they can be inexpensive sources of furniture. Obviously, the pieces that you find at car boot sales tend to be smaller – a local boot sale might be a good place to hunt for a Lloyd Loom wicker chair or laundry basket, but do not expect to find a Chippendale side chair or an oak dresser very often.

BUYING AT BOOT SALES

As always, the old adage 'the early bird catches the worm' holds true. Try to arrive at the boot sale as early as possible and always carry a torch. The light can be poor if it is early in the morning or late in the afternoon and you need to be able to inspect items closely before you part with any cash. Anyone who has ever sold at a boot sale will tell you that the first to arrive are the dealers (who may arrive well before dawn). They may not say much, but they sift carefully through the sale to find anything worth buying.

Bear in mind, if you find something that catches your eye, that the prices at a boot sale are usually flexible, so it really is worth bargaining (gently, but firmly) with the person selling. If you are hoping to buy at the fair, take coins and low value notes rather than credit cards and cheques, but remember to keep your money secure in an inside pocket or money belt. Also keep in mind that there has been an unfortunate increase in the amount of stolen property that is disposed of at boot sales. If you are in any doubt, ask a few questions about the provenance of the piece. You should also try to obtain a written receipt with the name and address of the person from whom you are buying. It is also a very good idea to note the registration number of the seller's car.

Lloyd Loom chairs often crop up at boot sales, frequently under large piles of junk!

SELLING AT BOOT SALES

If you intend selling at a boot sale, you will usually be charged an entrance fee according to the size of your vehicle. Again, arrive early to get a good position and to give yourself time to set up properly. It is worth packing the car the night before to make sure that everything you want to take fits. Also, decide what price you want for your property before you go to the sale and, if possible, mark each item with its price; this will save you having to make on-the-spot decisions that you might regret with hindsight.

BUYING FROM ADVERTISEMENTS

Classified advertisement columns in a wide variety of publications, including national newspapers, local papers and the specialist collector's magazines, can all be fruitful sources for buying and selling antiques.

If you spot an advertisement that looks promising, try to find out as much about the piece as possible before you make the journey to see it. Ask for the price and a full description, including size, wood, age (if it is known), condition and whether it has been repaired.

SELLING THROUGH ADVERTISEMENTS

If you are selling through an advertisement, make sure that you have a sound idea of the value of the piece before you place the advertisement. Show a photo or the object itself to a few reputable dealers or auction houses to get some idea of its market value. Look at descriptions of similar objects in auction house catalogues for an idea of how to describe the piece, word the advertisement clearly and succinctly, and always include the object's dimensions, its age (if you know it), and a note of any decoration that could make the piece more

If you want to find the best pieces, try to arrive at car boot sales before the dealers.

attractive to buyers. Your advertisement should include a box number or telephone number, but do not, in the interests of security, include your name or address.

If you include a telephone number, make sure that you are in when the advertisement first appears. Be prepared to name the price you are looking for (you should negotiate if necessary) and to give the prospective buyer a full description of the piece and its condition. If you manage to find a buyer, never part with your property before you have been paid in full with cash or the cheque has cleared.

PART 2

FURNITURE
CARE

ABOVE THE THIN WOOD USED FOR CHEST BACKS
IS EASILY DAMAGED.

LEFT THE CHOICE OF FURNITURE IN THIS
ROOM WAS INSPIRED BY THE COLLECTION OF
VICTORIAN PAINTINGS, MANY OF THEM BY
SIR LAWRENCE ALMA–TADEMA.

VALUING & INSURING

The increased awareness of the value of art and antiques has had one unfortunate drawback – the likelihood of burglary has never been higher. There is some good news for furniture collectors, however: because furniture is larger and heavier than most other antiques, it is less vulnerable to theft. On the other hand, furniture is bought to be used as well as admired, so it is more prone to any type of accidental damage than an antique that is kept safely in a display cabinet.

Adequate insurance is essential, since it protects not only against theft, but also against damage through fire and flood and so on. A valuation is also useful if you bought your collection many years ago and have no idea of its current market value.

Most insurance companies now call for a professional valuation for any object worth more than a certain sum, usually based on a percentage of your overall policy. You can set about having an insurance valuation carried out in several ways. Most insurance companies will accept valuations given by any reputable specialist – whether this person is an independent valuer, an auction house valuer, or even an individual dealer. If your collection happens to be specialized in one particular field, such as furniture, a specialist dealer will usually be very pleased to value its contents.

If you do not know any dealers, associations such as LAPADA or BADA can supply you with the names and telephone numbers of those in your area. However, responsibility for the accuracy of the valuation will be the dealer's alone.

Valuation documents are required by increasing numbers of insurance companies.

INSURANCE CHECKLIST

- CHOOSE A VALUER WHO IS SUITED TO YOUR TYPE OF COLLECTION
- MAKE SURE THAT THE VALUER IS ACCEPTABLE TO YOUR INSURER
- AGREE THE VALUATION FEE BEFOREHAND
- SHOP AROUND FOR YOUR INSURANCE
- HAVE YOUR VALUATION UPDATED REGULARLY

COST

The price that you have to pay for a valuation can vary considerably, so it is always worth shopping around for the best deal. The cost is calculated in one of three ways: as a percentage of the total value of the property involved (this is usually between ½ and 1½ per cent); on a daily rate, based on how long it takes the valuer to assess the property, plus additional travelling expenses; by the two parties agreeing a flat fee.

Before the valuer begins an assessment of your collection, you should also make clear at what level you want your property valued. If, for instance, you are happy to buy at auction, the amount that your collection or piece is insured for might be less than the 'retail replacement' figure (the price you would expect to pay if you bought from one of the well-known West End dealers). The insurance figure should be at least 20 per cent more than you would expect to receive if you sold the same item at an auction; in this way you take into account both the buyer's commission and the tax that you would pay.

This George III ormolu-mounted mahogany wine cooler, c.1765, was discovered on an insurance valuation by Bonhams. It later sold for £51,700.

THE VALUATION

Along with the figure an item of furniture is worth, the valuer should provide an accurate description and measurements of each object in your collection, with the date or approximate date the piece of furniture was made, the material (oak, say, or mahogany), and a note of decoration and defects it may have. Many valuers will also supply you with photographs of the objects they have valued. Keep these in a safe place, preferably not at home, together with the valuation, as they will be of invaluable help to the police in the event of theft. The valuation should also include the name, address and credentials of the company or individual who carried out the appraisal.

INSURING

Once your collection has been valued, how do you insure it? As with valuers, there is a range of insurers from which to choose, and it is always worth asking several companies for a quote based on your valuation. People often include their antiques on general household policies, but this is not necessarily the most cost-effective way to insure them. If you have a moderate-sized or even a relatively large collection, it may be worth investigating the charges of specialist art insurers who break antiques down into various categories according to the risk – furniture is charged at a lower rate than silver, which is more portable and incurs a higher risk of theft.

UP-DATING INSURANCE

Most valuers recommend that their estimates be revised every three to four years. The charge for up-dating will usually be a fixed fee that is considerably less than the initial cost of the valuation. It is worth having the figures professionally updated because certain types of furniture can increase dramatically in price – a good valuer will be sure to keep in touch with recent market trends.

SECURITY

Most theft is opportunistic. Unless you live in a particularly spectacular residence, a burglar who spots a wide open window or an unlocked door is far more likely to break into your home than the professional antiques snatcher. The best way to deter this type of theft is by making your home obviously uninviting. Window locks, good-quality locks on all your doors, effective burglar alarms, and bright security lights are all readily available for a moderate cost, and if you need advice on how to make your home more secure, talk to a Crime Prevention Officer. Your local police officers will advise you free of charge and recommend reputable specialist security firms who could carry out the work for you.

You can assist the recovery of your property by marking your furniture with a security pen. However, many collectors prefer not to mark their antiques in this way, because the pen is indelible and should you want to sell the item at a later date it could deter potential buyers.

Another way to protect your prized possessions is to make sure that you do not leave obviously valuable objects on display where they can be seen by all and sundry. When you go away on holiday, notify the local police so that they can keep an eye on your house and, if possible, hide any small or particularly precious pieces. You could place them in a bank safety-deposit box, and some banks will take a whole trunkful of valuables.

SECURITY CHECKLIST
- MAKE YOUR HOME UNINVITING TO BURGLARS
- TAKE EXTRA PRECAUTIONS WHEN YOU ARE AWAY ON HOLIDAY
- PHOTOGRAPH EVERYTHING OF VALUE IN YOUR COLLECTION
- DO NOT KEEP THE PHOTOS IN YOUR HOME
- KEEP AN UPDATED INVENTORY OF YOUR COLLECTION

PHOTOGRAPHING

Of all the ways of helping the police to recover your possessions should they be stolen, having good photographs is probably the most effective. Photographs of stolen antiques can be logged with the Art and Antiques Squad. This is a specialized police department that has a national database holding photographs and descriptions of property stolen anywhere in the country. If the effort of photographing your collection seems too much like hard work, bear in mind that should your property be stolen and the police be unable to identify its rightful owner, in many cases not only will the thief have evaded prosecution, he or she will also be able to take your property home.

Apart from the police, there are various other firms that can help to track down stolen antiques, but they all depend on having photographs. There is a specialist publication, *Trace*, that carries photographs of stolen items to dealers and salerooms. Photographs of stolen property are also published in the *Antiques Trade Gazette*. In addition, there is a database of stolen property called the Art Loss Register, which helps to trace stolen pieces that are sold through auction rooms and dealers both in this country and abroad.

You do not have to use a professional photographer to record your collection for the purposes of security. Provided that a few simple rules are followed, and that you possess a reasonable camera, you should be able to do it yourself. Unless you have an evenly-lit room (preferably one where the windows are not all on the same side), it is advisable to photograph as much of your collection as possible outdoors. However, with large pieces of furniture (dining tables, dressers, sideboards and so on) this may prove impractical.

Whether you are photographing inside or outside, choose a day when there is a light cloud cover, so that the shadows are soft. For the best results, use standard 35mm print film or the new improved polaroid camera (available on loan from some Crime Prevention Officers). Do not use the older type of polaroid camera as the images deteriorate and fade over a period of time.

To take the picture, stand with the sun behind you, level with the object and close enough for it nearly to fill the view-finder. Photograph small or very ornate objects against a plain background: white, black or grey are best (a large sheet is ideal). If you put a ruler beside each object, it will act as a scale reference.

Begin by photographing the object from the front and, then, from as many other angles as possible. Include close-up shots of any particularly distinctive decoration – for instance, any marquetry or carving on the legs and handles. Also take close-ups of any defects – chips, dents and scratches can all help to identify your chair or table from a mass of similar ones.

Once you have photographed your collection, it is a good idea to take general shots of the relevant rooms. This will help you to remember any smaller items that might otherwise be overlooked.

It is a wise precaution to have more than one set of photographs. Keep one set with your inventory and another at your bank or with your solicitor.

DOCUMENTING

Keeping an inventory together with your photographs will prove an invaluable source of reference, as well as being useful for security. As your collection grows you will find it an indispensable way of remembering the history of a piece. You should list:

● where each object came from – antique shop, auction, boot sale etc;
● the date you acquired it, with the price you paid and the full written receipt;
● a full visual description of the piece;
● a full condition report – note any cracks, chips, lifting veneers, replacement handles, areas of necessary restoration etc;
● anything else you know about the object's history and any correspondence relating to it. If you have taken the trouble to show it to an expert who has given you his or her written opinion on it, keep this useful information as well.

This 19th-century mahogany bergère could be easily transported by a burglar; always make sure that your home is as secure as possible.

DISPLAY

Flick through the pages of any good home furnishings magazine and the chances are that you will see numerous tastefully arranged rooms filled to the brim with antiques. Such interiors might seem to be the realms of millionaires and beyond your reach, but if you look closely at each piece of furniture individually, you might find that many are not such great rarities after all. It is the way in which the items of furniture are arranged that enhances their appearance, and that of other pieces in the room. It is quite possible to create a spectacular effect with very modest pieces of furniture − this is the art of successful display.

Deciding on where to place your carefully chosen antiques can be a problem for even the most confident collector, but a few simple guidelines can make displaying antiques one of the most enjoyable aspects of owning them.

Of course, displaying antiques is not simply a question of appearance. A well-arranged room has a harmonious elegance that not only looks good but also fits in with the practicalities of your day-to-day life, and, most importantly, conserves the antiques in good condition.

First of all, take into account your own requirements. For instance, you should not put delicate occasional tables in the way of toddlers or pets. You should then consider the furniture's well-being. Materials such as wood and papier mâché are particularly vulnerable to powerful sources of heat and light, so do not place furniture in front of radiators or in direct sunlight, since this can cause veneers to lift and wooden table tops to warp − these are problems that will probably prove expensive to rectify (see also p.34).

The way a piece of furniture was intended to be used should also help you decide where to put it. For example, some pieces, such as chests of drawers and bureaux, were made to stand against walls, and have unpolished panels at the back, or, at least, no decoration on one side. Such pieces are clearly best positioned as they were intended to be: against walls. If you put a chest in the middle of a room, no matter how beautiful it looks from the front, it will always look ugly from behind.

On the other hand, some pieces, such as circular tables, work tables and davenports, were made to be seen 'in the round'. These are finished on all sides, and you will be taking best advantage of their style if you place them in the centre of a room.

As you arrange the furniture in a room you should consider the overall effect as well as each piece individually. Creating separate groups of furniture and leaving space in between them, rather than simply arranging your pieces evenly around the walls, will break up the space into distinct areas and create several focuses of interest.

Whether your room is large or small, try to display some pieces symmetrically to give balance to the overall decorative

---

DISPLAY CHECKLIST

- POSITION THE PIECE SO THAT IT IS SEEN TO ITS BEST ADVANTAGE
- PROTECT FURNITURE FROM ANY SOURCES OF DIRECT HEAT AND LIGHT
- USE LARGER OR DECORATIVE PIECES TO CREATE FOCAL POINTS
- TRY TO MAKE A BALANCED ARRANGEMENT
- MAKE SURE THAT YOUR ROOM SETTING SUITS YOUR LIFESTYLE
- DO NOT OVER-FURNISH

scheme. Start with your largest or most imposing piece of furniture, such as a bureau or a sideboard, and emphasize its importance by placing it centrally against a wall and putting smaller pieces, say a pair of matching chairs or tables, on either side to frame the central focal point and to draw attention to it. If you do not have a pair of anything to arrange on either side of your centrally featured piece, try to balance smaller pieces of similar size and shape.

You can also draw attention to very decorative pieces of furniture by the way you display other objects in the room. For instance, a picture (or group of pictures) or a mirror above a desk or table will draw attention to it.

Another approach is to group decorative objects on a piece in order to highlight it. A pair of candlesticks or candelabra is a classic accompaniment to a sideboard, adding height and sparkle. If you have a collection of silver objects or boxes, it might be a good idea to display them on a small table. However, take care before standing objects on old furniture. Silver and metal items, particularly those with feet, can scratch the surfaces of the pieces they are placed on. If in doubt, put them on mats to protect the wood, or attach a small, self-sticking felt pad onto the bottom of each foot.

Do not forget the floor either – a small decorative

rug in front of a special piece of furniture will act as a magnet to the eye.

Lighting can play an important part in the display of antique furniture as well. A spotlight directed onto a bureau bookcase or a display cabinet will highlight its importance in a room setting and can emphasize the beautiful figuring of veneers. A pair of lamps on small tables on either side of an attractive sofa will serve as a practical aid to reading, as well as helping subtly to 'frame' the sofa.

Finally, the most difficult requirement for any keen furniture collector: remember not to over-furnish. Obviously, how much furniture to put in a room is largely a matter of personal taste, but bear in mind that if you over-furnish a room you will detract from everything in it and create an impression of overall clutter. Less is often more, so, if you find that you have too much to fit in your room, it might be time to consider selling two or three pieces and buying one of real quality – and starting to arrange your room again!

A strong, attractive wall colour makes this excellent George III sideboard really glow. The pair of George III knife boxes shows the Georgian flair for combining practicality with elegance.

CARE & RESTORATION

Looking after antique furniture correctly allows you to enjoy living with it, while at the same time conserving it in good condition. Most furniture that you are likely to come across (and that which is featured in this book) was robustly made and can endure reasonable use. Enjoying and using antique furniture is a fundamental reason for collecting it; there is no need to be afraid of furniture just because it is old. Do not forget that most pieces have survived several decades, if not centuries, of wear and should be able to last in reasonable condition well into the future, provided that you observe a few simple guidelines.

When you purchase a piece of antique furniture it is likely to be in less than perfect condition. Deciding how much 'wear and tear' is acceptable or whether the piece needs restoring is largely a matter of personal choice. The general rule of thumb, however, is: if in doubt, leave it alone. Restoration is very expensive and most antique furniture will outlive you with no more than a flick of a duster, but it will need attention if a piece is in a serious state of disrepair.

Drops of liquid left on a wooden surface do great harm. This is a detail from the water-stained dressing table that is illustrated on p.142.

HEAT & LIGHT

Excessive heat and strong sunlight are the two main enemies of antique furniture. Georgian craftsmen allowed for woods to expand and contract slightly, and to adapt slowly to the changes of the seasons; the modern combination of central heating and double-glazing, however, creates hot airless rooms without humidity. Invariably, this means that veneers split and planks warp. An ordinary humidifier available from most department stores will alleviate this problem to a large extent.

Do not place furniture in direct sunlight; diffuse it with a blind or place a protective cover on the furniture. Although gentle daylight mellows wood and helps to give it an attractive, soft patina, excessive sunlight dries the wood and can cause cracks and damage to veneers.

POLISHING & DUSTING

Polish antique furniture very sparingly (once a year is almost too much), using a proper bee's wax polish (ask your dealer to recommend a good brand); do not use too much polish because this clogs the wood and makes it sticky. Never use a silicone spray – this will coat the outside of a wood with a shiny seal while drying the inside. Dust your pieces regularly, but with great care, especially on veneered and inlaid items, as little raised bits of veneer are easily broken by careless dusting.

VENEERS & INLAYS

When small bits of inlay break off or come out, repair them immediately; otherwise you will be left with rough edges that flick up when you are dusting the piece. You should be able to stick small pieces back yourself – remember to clean out any old glues first and to use a wood glue, not a modern adhesive.

Take care with veneers and inlays. This table is missing some pieces, which probably came off when the piece was dusted too vigorously.

WOODWORM

Wood-boring beetles such as the *Anobium punctatum* are, depressingly, almost impossible to treat properly. Although fumigation will help, these grubs are capable of going dormant after treatment, and when they wake up they will attack something untreated. Never underestimate the gravity of woodworm: you might only see half a dozen holes, but underneath there may be a maze of tunnels that will seriously weaken the structure of the wood.

If you see evidence of tunnels on the surface, this means the wood has been planed down, and was probably originally from another piece. In order to identify active woodworm, examine the holes in spring, when the grubs are active: dust around the holes or on the floor means the grubs are active. Woodworm normally attacks softwoods, such as pine or beech. The beech seat rails of 18th-century chairs are particularly vulnerable. If a chair has been re-railed, woodworm is usually the reason for it. Woodworm rarely attacks hardwoods such as mahogany, but it can attack a softwood carcass veneered with mahogany, in which case flight holes (caused when the beetle hatches and leaves the wood) may appear.

HANDLING & MOVING

Moving carved or veneered furniture can be especially hazardous to its welfare, since rapid changes in atmosphere and temperature can quickly cause veneers to lift. Few furniture warehouses have proper temperature control; the best are brick buildings, as these heat up and cool down gradually. If you are moving, be sure that you do not let carriers leave expensive pieces of furniture out in direct sunlight even for just a few moments.

When moving furniture:
• have two people rather than one for each piece and lift rather than drag it;
• support case furniture by its framework, never use carrying handles;
• lift chairs by their seat rails, not by their backs;
• lift tables by their under-frames or bases rather than by their tops.

PART 3

FURNITURE

FUNDAMENTALS

LEFT THE VENEER AND MARQUETRY ON THIS
SUPERB MAHOGANY BOOKCASE MAKE IT AN
EXTREMELY DESIRABLE PIECE. £4,500–6,000

ABOVE SMALL FURNITURE, SUCH AS THIS KNIFE BOX,
IS ALWAYS VERY COLLECTABLE. £400–600

WOODS

The understanding and appreciation of woods are fundamental to learning about and enjoying furniture. It is the enormous variety of grain and colour, together with years of polishing and fading, that give woods their patinations – a large contributing factor to the value of a good piece.

Developing a knowledge of which woods were used and when is, in my opinion, the basis of learning how to date and recognize the style of a piece. It is much easier to learn to identify polished rather than unpolished woods, since most woods look completely different when polished.

AMBOYNA
Pterospermun indicum

A Regency teapoy.

Imported from the West Indies in the 18th century, amboyna was used as veneers on expensive furniture. It was rarely used in the last 20 years of the 18th century, but is found on pieces made in the Regency period and the Continental Empire period.

ASH
Fraxinus excelsior
An indigenous wood that was used (always in the solid) for cheap country furniture; it was at its height from 1750 to 1850. It is not suitable for carving

and very vulnerable to woodworm.

BEECH
Fagus sylvatica

An 18th-century French caned beechwood chair.

This is an indigenous wood used in the solid on country furniture from the 17th century onwards (especially for chair frames). Beech is easy to carve and almost all French chair frames are made from it, whether they are

polished, painted or gilt. It has been used for wooden spoons and other kitchen utensils, as well as for the handles of tools and brushes. It is less common in North American furniture.

BIRCH
Betula alba

This pale indigenous wood was used for country furniture from the 17th century onwards but few early examples survive. It is mainly seen in the solid or as veneers on Austro-German Biedermeier furniture that was made between 1800 and 1930. The best birch is called 'Satin birch' and was occasionally used as an outside veneer in the late 18th century. From c.1850 to 1900, it was commonly used as a lining for work boxes. Figured birch can be mistaken for satinwood when used on the fronts of chests.

BOXWOOD
Buxus sempervirens
A hard, slow-growing, light-coloured, indigenous wood, with

a fine close grain, boxwood was used in the 16th and 17th centuries for inlay turning. It was used in the 18th century for inlay and, from 1770 to 1820, for stringing. The Bible mentions boxwood combs, spinning tops and writing tables. More recently, it has been used for engravers' blocks, rulers and shuttles, and tools for the weaving and silk industries.

CALAMANDER
Diospyros quaesita

A cabinet, c.1890, with doors crossbanded in calamander.

Imported from Sri Lanka (of the same family as ebony), this hardwood was used as veneers and for crossbanding in the Regency period, and also on small boxes.

CEDAR
Juniperus virginiana
From the United States, as well as the West Indies and Honduras,

this is a hard, durable, reddish-coloured, aromatic, worm-resistant wood that was used from c.1770 to 1820 for drawer linings on quality furniture and storage chests. It was favoured because it is said to repel insects. While the wood is not particularly strong, it is noted for having a very high resistance to decay.

CHERRY

Prunus cerasus/ Prunus avium

An indigenous, warm reddish-coloured wood occasionally used for inlay in the 17th century and in the solid in mid-18th-century North American furniture. It was used in France from c.1750 for provincial pieces.

COROMANDEL

Diospyros melanoxylon
This is imported from the Coromandel coast of India. A very heavy, fine-grained hardwood like ebony, which is striped like calamander wood; it is sometimes called Zebra wood.

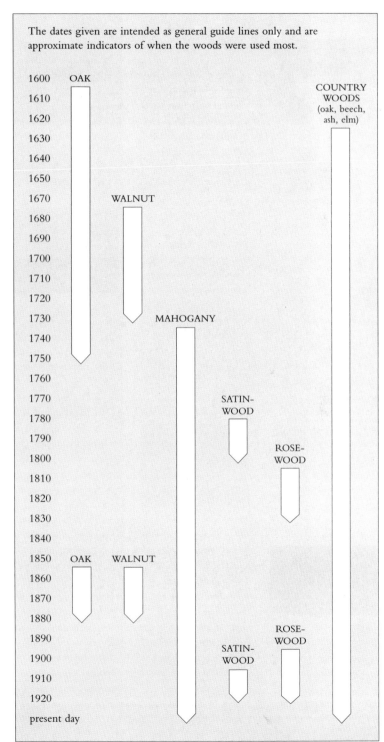

The dates given are intended as general guide lines only and are approximate indicators of when the woods were used most.

EBONY
Diospyros

A 19th-century Anglo-Indian ebony and exotic wood table.

Ebony is a very hard, fine-grained wood that grows in tropical climates. It was used for veneers on cabinets and mirrors in the 17th century and especially favoured during the Regency period. Its black tone was copied in English 'ebonized' and French *bois noircie* (black-painted) pieces of the 19th century.

ELM
Ulmus procera

Elm is an indigenous, medium-brown, coarsely grained wood that looks similar to oak but is much softer and more susceptible to worm. It was used for country chairs, especially for the seats of Windsor chairs in the 18th century, and for other large country pieces throughout the 19th century. Elm's appearance, with a prominent growth-ring figure, has a coarse texture and an often irregular grain. The wood is pale brown, sometimes with a reddish tint or, as in wych elm, a greenish cast. In general, elm is not a strong wood but is quite water-resistant. Elm is the traditional wood for coffins in some countries but it is rarely used for any furniture in America.

KINGWOOD
Dalbergia

Kingwood is a stripy-grained wood from Brazil, used extensively in France from the early 18th century to c.1780 for quality pieces of parquetry. Side panels and drawers were often quarter-veneered with grains radiating from the centre. In England it was sparingly used in the 17th and late 18th centuries, when it was known as 'Prince's wood'. It was used in England and France between about 1840 and 1860, during the revival of Louis XV furniture, a style that the Victorians found very attractive.

MAHOGANY
Swietenia

There are two main types of mahogany: Cuban and Honduran. Cuban mahogany is the rarer of the two and was chiefly used before c.1750. Its darker tone is generally only seen on expensive pieces. Mahogany's popularity during the 18th century was based on the fact that it is easy to carve, resistant to worm and fairly stable. It was used both as a veneer and in the solid. In some of the poorer country areas, oak and elm were stained with ox blood to resemble mahogany; red walnut has also been used as a substitute. Continental European mahogany was usually from Haiti and has a distinctive grain. Although it was rarely used until the late 18th century, it was very popular in France during the Empire period; it was also used from the late 18th century in Germany and Denmark. In the 20th century many timbers with similar qualities have been used as substitutes for mahogany.

OAK
Quercus

There are various oaks, both indigenous and imported. The mainstay of English furniture until the end of the 17th century, oak was used for country pieces until the 20th century. From the late 17th century, it was used as a carcass wood; after c.1800 carcasses were often made from a combination of oak and pine. During the Victorian period, oak was used for sideboards and for many Gothic Revival pieces. Oak is a strong, durable wood that resists damp and worm much better than, say, elm; initially, however, the two are easily confused.

PINE
Pinus

19th-century pine, recently stripped and polished.

Indigenous to Europe, this straight-grained wood was easy to carve and was used as a base for gilt mirrors. In provincial areas in the early 18th century, it was sometimes used for the sides of walnut pieces and stained to match. It was also used as a base for painted and japanned furniture and more commonly from c.1800 as a carcass wood, especially for the backs of pieces of case furniture. During the 19th century, cheaper pieces for the bedroom and kitchen were made from pine that had been painted. The most common of the various types of pine is the European redwood, which is also known as the 'Scots' pine. It is available in central Europe and Asia, as well as in Scandinavia. In North America, hard yellow and white pine were used as secondary woods.

ROSEWOOD
Dalbergia nigra

This is a richly coloured wood with striped grain that was used in the 17th century for decoration, and in the Chippendale period as a veneer on French-style furniture. Most popular from 1800 to 1840 and from 1870 to 1900, it was also used by French Art Deco *ébenistes*.

SATINWOOD
Chloroxylon swietenia/Xanthoxylun flavium

Most 18th-century satinwood came from the West Indies. Satinwood has been popular in England at a number of times: during the Sheraton period from 1790 to 1800, at the time of the Regency Revival of the 1880s, and during the Edwardian era, from 1900 to 1914. It was usually used as veneers.

TULIPWOOD
Dalbergia

A detail from a 19th-century French tulipwood-veneered writing table.

This wood, imported from Brazil and used for veneers and crossbanded borders, often appears on quality French furniture, usually in conjunction with kingwood. In England, it was often used as crossbanding for rosewood.

WALNUT
Juglans regia/ Juglans nigra

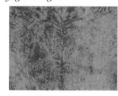

An indigenous wood that was used in England and France from the Renaissance onwards. Trees that were planted in Queen Elizabeth I's reign were culled a century later at the height of the fashion for walnut. It is noted for its excellent finish. The wood was good for carving, although susceptible to worm attack. It was used both in the solid and as a veneer for the earliest case furniture, until it was supplanted by mahogany c.1750. It was equally prized in continental Europe. Fine Italian, French and German furniture in the 16th and 17th centuries commonly made use of walnut. It returned to favour in the Victorian period, from 1850 to 1880. The range and variety of cuts and grains can be confusing, and polished walnut can look black.

YEW
Taxus

A hard, reddish-toned indigenous wood that was occasionally used in the 17th century (and until about 1730) as a veneer. Quality provincial furniture was often made from solid yew and it was always used for the arms of high-quality Windsor chairs. It is sometimes used today to make reproduction pieces.

CONSTRUCTION

An understanding of how furniture was made in different periods is extremely valuable both for dating a piece and for deciding where the item was made.

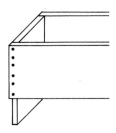

Boarded or planked construction.

Early furniture was made from planks of wood that were nailed together (as shown above).

Joined construction.

On later, more refined furniture, a framework joined by mortise and tenon joints, held in place by wooden dowel pegs or 'trenails', and filled with panels became usual (shown above). This method is found on coffers, settles and chests of drawers made before 1700. The vertical boards that

become the legs are called stiles; the horizontal members are called rails. Dowels were used less in the 18th century as glues improved. Old dowels stand 'proud' beyond the joint because wood shrinks across the grain over time.

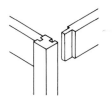

An example of a mortise and tenon joint.

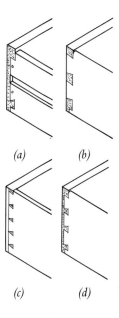

(a) *(b)*

(c) *(d)*

Illustrations showing the development of dovetail joints from the late 17th century to the early 18th century.

On hand-cut dovetails, the scribing line is often quite visible.

From the latter part of the 17th century onwards, dovetail joints were used in case furniture such as chests of drawers and cupboards. At first drawers were crudely made, often nailed together with a groove on each side to allow the drawer to slide *(a)*. By c.1700 *(b)*, under the influence of Dutch craftsmen, dovetails became finer and more sophisticated. As the 18th century progressed, dovetails on top-quality pieces became finer still *(c)*, while on country pieces of a similar date they may be relatively crude *(d)*. By the 20th century, the more sophisticated workshops were using machinery to produce dovetails. Most 18th-century drawer linings were made from oak. By 1800, pine was being used increasingly (it was cheaper) and dovetails were often less sophisticated.

LATER CONSTRUCTION

Note how the prongs on machine-cut dovetails such as this are the same size as the insets.

Although machines were used in furniture construction from the 1830s, it was not until electricity became widespread in Europe in the early 20th century that machine-made dovetails prevailed – and even then only in bigger workshops that could afford the machines. Machine-cut dovetails are easy to identify because the prongs are the same size as the insets, and because there is never a scribing line. Another way of dating a piece is to examine the grain. The grain is the general direction of the wood's fibres. In the 18th century, most English drawer bottoms had the grain running from back to front as shown above. To help you remember, there is a useful phrase 'long

before 1750'. (In North America, where wood was plentiful, this rule is less true.)

SCREWS

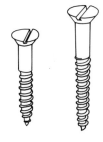

The head of a handmade screw, from before c.1850, is off-centre (left). The head of a machine-made screw, from after c.1850, is perfectly centred (right).

Early screws were handmade from iron and have uneven threads. They were not tapered as much as modern screws, and can be difficult to extract if they have rusted in. Note that the groove in the screw head is placed slightly off-centre.

NAILS

Early nails, known as 'clout' nails, have narrow heads and were handmade so each is slightly different in size. By the mid-18th century, nails were stamped from metal sheets, so they became more uniform in size and have regular machine-made heads. The heads of early clout nails have five distinct surfaces where the molten top of the nail was hit five times to make the flower-shaped head. Old nails, however, can be difficult to identify; viewed from the top, a rusted modern upholstery tack with a reshaped head is virtually the same as an old five clout or so-called 'rose-head' nail.

CHAIRS

This 18th-century chair has an open corner brace.

Early chair seat frames had blocks glued to their corners. By 1700, frames were given open corner braces, usually glued or nailed from one seat rail to the other, leaving an open triangle between

A 19th-century chair with a filled bracket.

the brace and leg. From c.1850, the Victorians returned to an improved version of the 17th-century idea, using a filled block or bracket always glued and screwed. Victorian repairers often replaced the open Georgian bracket with the block system, leaving the tell-tale marks of the earlier construction. The shape of corner blocks provides a clue to when a chair was made. Victorian blocks are usually convex, while 20th-century blocks tend to be larger and concave.

STRETCHERS

A round-turned stretcher going into a square block on the leg (as above) usually denotes continental manufacture – English chairs of early date or of provincial origin usually have legs joining stretchers of matching form. Many chairs have stretchers joining all four legs together, but, by the time of Queen Anne, better London cabinet-makers were able to make seat rails with sufficient strength not to require the additional support of stretchers, thus giving a less cluttered and more flowing line to the legs.

TABLES

Tables in the 17th century were made from planks often held together with cleats – strips of wood that were fastened to the ends. Look carefully on plank tops for unexplained marks (nail holes) that might indicate that the wood came from floorboards. Most dining tables are made from solid wood and large mahogany tables usually have the grain running widthways across the table. Table tops are very often married to later bases, and you should take the trouble to look underneath for evidence of holes or colour changes that could indicate where a different base was once attached.

DETAILS & DECORATION

The way in which a piece of furniture is decorated can have a major effect on its desirability and value, as well as helping with dating. Some of the most popular methods of decorating furniture are outlined below.

CARVING

Detail of the back of an early 20th-century Jacobean-style chair – if this were a genuine 17th-century example, the pierced areas would be sharply angled inwards.

Carving was one of the most popular ways of decorating furniture and was widely used throughout the centuries. The fineness of the detail depends to some extent on the grain of the wood, but also on the expertise of the carver. In the 17th and 18th centuries, the effect of intricate pierced

carving was lightened by under-cutting: the back of the design was angled inwards. In late 19th- to early 20th-century copies of earlier carving there is little or no under-cutting, so the overall effect is noticeably heavier. Carving is not always contemporary with the piece; in the late Victorian and Edwardian period early plain furniture, especially oak, was often 'improved' with later carving.

VENEERS
The technique of veneering which involves covering a carcass with a thin layer of attractively grained, more expensive wood, was imported to England by Dutch craftsmen in the late 17th century. Early veneers were cut in a saw pit, and vary in thickness between ⅟₁₆in and ⅛in (1.6mm and 1.4mm). All modern veneers will be under ⅟₁₆in (1.6mm) thick if cut with a circular saw, and paper thin if machine planed. From the mid-18th century onwards, band saws allowed more even and

slightly thinner veneers to be cut. Once the thin layers of veneer have been cut, they can be laid in a variety of ways to create a decorative effect. One of the most popular types of veneering is quarter-veneering, in which four sheets are sliced in succession from one block, and the sheets are laid together to create a pattern. Veneers may be cut from the tree in various ways: if they are cut lengthways, the grain will be longitudinal; if they are cut across the roots a burr effect is achieved; if cut across the top where the tree was pollarded, another variation occurs. Drawer fronts and the edges of chests are often crossbanded; this involved edging the main veneered surface with sections cut at right angles to the centre.

Cross- and feather-banding on a walnut-veneered drawer front, c.1720.

INLAY
The crudest form of inlay is when a shape is gouged out of a wooden surface and pieces of coloured woods are inserted to make a pattern. This form of decoration was used on English and continental furniture from the 17th century onwards and on American furniture from the 18th century.

MARQUETRY

A mid-18th-century Dutch bureau cabinet with later marquetry. (Marquetry was always added later on 18th-century pieces.)

This refinement of the same technique involves cutting shapes in a veneer. Marquetry decoration first became popular in England in the late 17th century, with the influx of Dutch craftsmen, following

of the late 17th century uses a marquetry of brass and tortoiseshell (see p.125).

PARQUETRY

The fine-quality parquetry adds greatly to the value of this 19th-century table.

Parquetry is a type of marquetry decoration in which the whole surface of the wood is made up of separate geometrically shaped pieces of wood (like a parquet floor). Because of its elaborate nature, parquetry tends to be found on smaller furniture, especially Regency tables and tea caddies. It was popular in England during the 17th and early 19th centuries and also found favour in continental Europe.

NATURAL COLOUR
Taste varies, but most English collectors prefer furniture with a rich colour that has built up over the years. This effect, called patina, is achieved

partly by the build-up of wax and dirt and partly by handling and polishing, and is, as a result, very difficult to fake or reproduce. This well-worn appearance is not as popular in continental Europe, where furniture is often stripped down, sanded and repolished to give an almost 'new' look. Beware, however: pieces of English furniture that have been repolished are often devalued in the English market.

FRENCH POLISH

A French polished door – the white flecks of the chalk base show through.

Old furniture was originally very brightly coloured; the red of 18th-century mahogany would be shocking to modern taste. Wood was usually coated in a spirit resin and a hardening oil that were used together in a French polish; waxes were also used.

Towards the end of the Victorian period and in the early 20th century, the demand for a high gloss finish led to much 18th-century furniture being French polished. This involved stripping away the old varnish, filling the grain with a chalky substance, and repolishing; with use, the whitish/yellowish chalk shows through the varnish. French polished furniture needs regular stripping-back; unfortunately, this is not a good idea – if it is done too often you will literally wear away the wood or veneer. A good professional restorer will be able to renew finishes and recreate patinas.

GILDING
Gilding is applied to a carved softwood frame, usually beech or pine. There are four stages to the process: first, the wood is sealed and made perfectly smooth with a chalky layer of gesso; second, a layer of red or yellow pigment, known as 'bole', is applied to give depth and richness to the gilding; third, the gold leaf is applied with a brush and glued in place with size (boiled linseed and turpentine); finally, the desired shine is created by burnishing

(rubbing) with an agate (an impure form of quartz). Other methods achieve slightly different results; water gilding, for example, where the gold leaf is applied to the clay bole with a gilder's sable tip, gives a brighter finish. As with patination, the requirements for regilding vary. In America, almost any piece is imperfect if regilded. Good new gilding is difficult to achieve, as it can look too harsh; it should always be undertaken by a qualified expert.

LACQUER
Lacquered furniture was made in the Orient by a lengthy process in which the surface of the wood is coated with layers of resin from the lac tree. This forms a shiny surface that is then decorated in a variety of ways (gold leaf, gesso etc.). Lacquer reached the Western world in the latter half of the 17th century, and became fashionable. The demand inspired European japanning, a painted imitation of the technique. Oriental lacquer panels were often incorporated into European furniture.

STYLES

BAROQUE

A carved beech stool, c.1690.

Originally a derogatory term derived from the Italian word *barroco*, meaning a misshapen pearl, baroque furniture is typically lavishly decorated with heavy carving, often including figural sculpture, cupids and curving shapes. The baroque style prevailed throughout continental Europe in the late 17th and early 18th centuries. Key designers of the period include Daniel Marot in Holland and England, Andrea Brustolon in Venice, and Jean Le Pautre in France.

QUEEN ANNE

Uncluttered elegance and restraint are associated with the reign of Queen Anne (1702–14). Walnut was the prevailing wood of the period and cabriole legs made their first appearance. Chairs with these cabriole legs, as well as vase-shaped splats, curved backs, and rounded stiles, are the elements that best epitomize the Queen Anne style.

ROCOCO

A giltwood pier mirror in rococo style.

Developed in France in the early 18th century, the word 'rococo' comes from the French *rocaille*, which means a fancy stonework and shellwork for fountains and grottoes. Rococo furniture is typified by a lighter, more fanciful, decorative style than baroque, which came before it. Asymmetrical ornament is typical of rococo; favourite motifs include shells, ribbons and flowers. The rococo style spread throughout Europe between c.1740 and 1760. The designs in Thomas Chippendale's Directory of 1754 reflect the English vogue that emerged for the French, Chinese and Gothic tastes. There was a departure from classical order and a move towards fantasy and asymmetry.

LOUIS XV

A Louis XV painted armchair, c.1760.

The French high rococo style is synonymous with the early part of the reign of Louis XV, whose name is associated with curving shapes and asymmetric forms. Comfort became an important consideration, and the bergère was one of many chair forms to evolve. Chinoiserie and Oriental motifs were very popular in this period. Leading cabinet-makers included Jean-François Oeben, Bernard II van Reisenburgh and Charles Cressent.

NEO-CLASSICISM

An 18th-century shield-back mahogany armchair.

Interest in the new discoveries made at Herculaneum and Pompeii in Italy combined with a reaction to rococo exuberance to create a new style that dominated the second half of the 18th century. It was pioneered in England in the work of Robert Adam, and is also reflected in the designs of Hepplewhite and Sheraton. Neo-classical furniture is typically decorated with classical motifs, such as masks, swags and columns. Carving is in low relief and usually symmetrical. The furniture is characteristically light and elegant in appearance. Straight, tapering legs are typical of chairs at this time as are geometrical forms and the use of Greek and Roman ornament.

LOUIS XVI

A Louis XVI beechwood fauteuil, c.1785.

In France the neo-classical style partially overlapped the reign of Louis XVI, whose name is associated with furniture made from his accession until the Revolution (1789). In contrast to Louis XV, lines became straighter and more rectilinear. Upholstered chairs typically had padded oval backs and straight, tapered and fluted legs. Giltwood and painted furniture was popular, as were marquetry, exotic woods, lacquer, *pietre dure*, and figurative bronze mounts. Leading cabinet-makers included Georges Jacob, with makers such as Jean-François Oeben and Jean-Henri Riesener working in the rococo and the classical periods as well as in the intermediate 'transitional' style when rococo curves started to straighten.

GEORGIAN

A loose term applied to anything made during the reign of the first three king Georges (c.1715–1820). The period encompasses rococo, neo-classical, and Regency styles and was one in which the leading designers, such as William Kent, Thomas Chippendale, and Thomas Hope, had an increasingly powerful impact on furniture styles of the day through their design books.

REGENCY

A Regency chair, c.1815.

A term used to describe not only furniture made in the reign of the Prince of Wales as Regent (1811–20), but the new style that evolved from c.1790 and remained fashionable until c.1830. Compared with the furniture of the preceding neo-classical period, styles became heavier and more sober, inspired by classical prototypes, such as the klismos chair and the X-framed stool. The decorative motifs were drawn from Ancient Egypt, Greece and Rome. The key designers were Thomas Sheraton, Thomas Hope, Henry Holland and George Smith. The term 'Regency' should not be confused with the French *régence* style, which refers to a pre-rococo style of furniture made in the early 18th century. Mahogany was the favourite wood but rosewood, zebrawood and maple veneers were also used.

EMPIRE

The French equivalent of the Regency style became synonymous in France with the reign of Napoleon between 1804 and 1815. Only very simple lines and minimal ornament were used. Marquetry and carving were replaced by metal mounts, often in the form of either swans, military motifs – such as wreaths, eagles and trophies – or bees. Leading furniture designers of the period included Charles Percier and Pierre-François Fontaine.

VICTORIAN

An octagonal walnut Victorian library table, c.1860, by the English makers Gillow.

A wide variety of styles enjoyed a revival of popularity in the reign of Queen Victoria; much of the furniture produced at this time exhibits a hybrid of neo-Gothic, rococo and neo-classical forms. However, the Victorians kept a style popular even when they had discovered a new one, whereas in the 18th century one style superseded another. The decoration of Victorian furniture is often elaborate with a profusion of carving; inlay and metal mounts were popular and often made by industrial machines. The later Victorian style took in the Aesthetic Movement (epitomized by the 'Japanese' designs of E.W. Godwin), the Arts & Crafts period (see p.123) and Art Nouveau – all of which helped to drive out overly fussy Victorian ornamentation.

COPIES, FAKES & ALTERATIONS

ALTERATIONS

A mahogany bureau bookcase, c.1780, which has 1880s inlay and stringing.

Over the years, many pieces of furniture have been altered, often quite simply to adapt them to a more useful purpose. Typical alterations of this type include large dining tables made into smaller breakfast tables, pole screens cut down and made into small wine tables, and tallboys divided into two chests. There are also conversions, such as Uncle Harry cutting the legs down to make a coffee table! At the top end of the market, an altered piece will be less desirable than, and only a fraction of the value of, one that has survived in pristine original condition; among the more

functional and less exclusive pieces a practical alteration may have little bearing on price. A commode made into a bedside table will not be worth much less than one with all its fittings because commodes are not generally used today and there is always a demand for bedside cabinets. The bottom of a dresser used as a server can have considerable value.

A mahogany tripod table, c.1750. This table now measures 1 ft 11 in (58cm) high and has been reduced in height to make a convenient side table.

Alterations such as changes to handles and feet are also common. Although it is obviously preferable to have the originals, replacements are acceptable if they are in keeping with the style of the piece. If the alterations are incongruous to the style it is definitely worth the effort and

money to restore the piece to the correct style. You will enhance its value as well as reviving its original appearance.

Queen Anne bureau cabinet, c.1700. The top and bottom are of similar date but did not start life together – a 'marriage'.

Another common alteration, which was much favoured by the Victorians and Edwardians, was later decoration. Many plain mahogany pieces had crossbanding, often in satinwood, and inlay added, while oak coffers were jazzed up with carved decoration, which often included spurious dates and initials. Alterations of this type generally have little bearing on price. While purists might understandably avoid later decorated pieces,

these items will nearly always find a home.

Some alterations were made to make furniture more comfortable. It is not uncommon to find 18th-century oval-backed upholstered chairs that have been fitted with spring-upholstered seats in the 19th or 20th centuries. Again, value will not be dramatically affected unless the springs alter the profile of the chair. More problematic are alterations made to enhance the value of a piece – for example, a cupboard that has had its original doors removed and has been fitted with glazed doors or a large dresser that has been cut down to a smaller size to make it more valuable. Square drop-leaf tables have been turned into more costly round ones; American gate-leg tables have been given rare butterfly-shaped supports to make them more valuable; plain-top tea tables have been given dished or pie crust edges. These pieces are much less desirable than their genuine counterparts and show the importance of checking furniture for signs of tampering before you buy.

MARRIAGES

A satinwood marquetry display cabinet that was made c.1900 in the George III style.

'Marriage' is a term used to describe a piece made from two or more parts that did not start life together. One of the most common of these is the small 18th-century bureau that has had a later bookcase added, or perhaps has had an approximately contemporary bookcase altered to fit it. Dressers with racks and tops and bottoms of tables are also frequent candidates for marriage. Standing back to look at the overall appearance of a piece is a good way to spot a marriage, as the proportions usually look wrong and give the game away. On a dresser or bureau bookcase, look closely at the sides: the wood should be of approximately the same grain and colour. Also look for similar mouldings, details and hardware on top and bottom. The boards on the back of the top and base should be the same if they came from the same place. Look underneath tables for unexplained holes – a clue to a replaced top.

REPRODUCTIONS

Most people now understand the term 'reproduction' in a purely derogatory sense; it misleadingly implies a 'fake' and suggests something that is rather inferior to an 'original'. Nevertheless, much very fine reproduction furniture was produced between the wars and since World War II, and it is now becoming popular. The best pieces reproduce not only design, but also the original proportions and construction. Some reproductions are artificially patinated and distressed to give a semblance of age, but, critically, there is no real attempt to pass the piece off as a genuine antique object.

Interestingly, the second-division status that is awarded to reproductions is a relatively recent phenomenon. In the 19th century, it was quite acceptable for a grand collector, if he could not obtain antique pieces, to have them copied. One of the most notable exemplars of this was the 4th Marquis of Hertford, founder of the Wallace Collection in London, who from the 1840s onwards had numerous copies of grand French royal furniture made, including the famous Bureau du Roi at Versailles. Much reproduction furniture of the inter-war period was scaled down to fit smaller modern living spaces. In general, it would be difficult to mistake honest reproductions as antiques, but, as these are used over the years, they will acquire the patina of age.

FAKES

A piece made by a cabinet-maker with intent to deceive is a fake. An increasing number of 'fakes' were, however, intended as faithful reproductions and have been passed on by a less than scrupulous third party as 'antique' or original. In recent years, as the demand for antique furniture has risen, more deliberate fakes have appeared in shops and auction rooms. Unfortunately, there are no easy answers to the problem of fakes: some are so carefully made that even the most expert eye would not necessarily be suspicious. Always take time to examine a piece carefully, in good light, and try to build up your experience through 'hands-on' contact with as much furniture as possible. Many reproductions are artificially distressed to give the appearance of age, but look closely and you will see that the wear tends to be unrealistically evenly distributed. A genuine antique would look most battered around the base and feet. Painted decoration can fool even seasoned collectors. Generally, the faker will decorate the front of a chest or box and then leave the sides a solid colour, something the more careful 18th- or 19th-century decorator would not have dreamt of doing. If in doubt, scientific tests can be used to determine the true age of paint, varnish and shellac.

PART 4

FURNITURE

FILE

LEFT NOTE THE SHERATON REVIVAL-STYLE INLAY
ON THIS EDWARDIAN MAHOGANY CORNER
WRITING-DISPLAY CABINET, A TYPICAL FEATURE
OF THIS PERIOD. £2,000–3,000

ABOVE A VICTORIAN MAHOGANY AND
EMBROIDERED SCREEN, c.1894. £2,250–3,000

The basic coffer is a simple box constructed from planks of wood with a hinged lid. But even though they were so simply made, coffers were (and still are) surprisingly versatile. In medieval times they were used for storing and transporting goods but also served as a seat or a side table. Today, they have additional uses that were unknown to our ancestors. For example, such furniture can provide a handy place for either sitting by the telephone or resting a television.

Most coffers and early chests were made from solid oak or walnut and decorated with carved or painted embellishment.

Early chests that were used for storing grain are called 'arks'; they have rounded lids that can be removed and reversed for kneading dough. The Yorkshire surname 'Arkwright' was given to the makers of this type of chest.

During the 18th century a wider variety of chest was made. It was not only the woods that changed, but the shapes too: you will find walnut-veneered chests made early in the century, followed by mahogany chests (those with serpentine shapes are especially valuable). There are also striking chests-on-stands and chests-on-chests. The most expensive distant cousins of the humble chest are American high chests and lavish English commodes. Some of these are valuable treasures that can cost tens of thousands of pounds.

COFFERS

The main disadvantage of the coffer is that anything resting on top of one has to be removed before the lid can be opened. For this reason, prices for coffers have tended to lag behind those of chests. Plain coffers made in the 17th and 18th centuries can be found for between £300 and £500, while coffers with elaborate original carving or painted decoration might cost £1,000 plus.

Because coffers were made over a long period, there are many variations in shape and design. By the mid-17th century, some coffers had drawers at their bases to make it easier to find things stored at the bottom; coffers of this type, sometimes called 'mule chests', evolved into chests of drawers.

▲ **CONSTRUCTION**
Coffers are difficult to date accurately because, while some joiners adopted new means of construction, others clung to more traditional techniques. The most basic coffer construction, using six planks – top, bottom, front, back and sides – held together with wooden dowels or nails, dates from 1600, or even earlier. Later, a framed construction connected with mortise and tenon joints was more commonly employed (see p.42). Made c.1675–1700 in Westmorland in England, this one combines old and new methods of construction with plank sides and a panelled front and top.
£1,400–1,800

◀ A TOUCH OF CLASS
In the late 19th and early 20th centuries, early coffers were sometimes recarved. Evening classes in wood carving were popular and couples often took along a family coffer to practice on. This 18th-century mule chest was decorated and dated in the late 19th century. Dates on chests can be particularly misleading. Pieces were often inscribed with an earlier date, or a coffer given as a marriage gift was carved with initials and the date, years after it was made.
£500–800

WHAT TO LOOK FOR
As with most coffers, this one (right) made c.1625–50 has iron hinges and locks. Before buying a coffer make sure that:
• the hinges are in good condition and the locks are original;
• inside, the wood is dry and has not been tampered with;
• the legs have not been replaced. If the coffer is of framed construction, the legs and the sides of the frame will be all one piece.
£2,000–3,000

◀ BONNET CHESTS
Although this chest looks as though it could be a dresser base or a double chest, in fact it is a bonnet chest made from solid mahogany c.1760. The top two rows of drawers are false and the hinged top opens to give plenty of room for storing hats (hence the name). A rising lid normally reduces value but this one is so unusual that the piece would be worth £2,000 to £2,500.

EARLY CHESTS OF DRAWERS

Chests were made in huge numbers from the late 17th century onwards, and even early ones are fairly easy to find today. Before you buy a chest, first pull out the drawers and examine the sides very carefully – their construction can tell you when the chest was made (see also p.42). During the 17th and 18th centuries dovetails on drawers were cut by hand; you might find four or five dovetail joints and you should be able to make out the scribing line along the outer side of the drawer that marked the depth to which the cabinet-maker had to cut.

DOVETAILS

Handmade   Machine-made

If the dovetails are the same width as the sections between them, they are probably machine-made – a 20th century feature.

◀ HANDLES
The bun feet, bobbin-turned decoration and geometric moulding on this typical c.1660 chest are original and as they should be; the handles, however, are out of place – you can see the shadows where the original pear drop handles once were (see p.48). Even so, they are not worth changing, as you would be left with even more marks. The good colour of the wood makes up for this fairly common defect.
£2,000–3,000

▶ FEET
Although oak is a very resilient wood, the feet of chests of drawers are susceptible to damage and are often replaced. If the replaced feet are in keeping with the style of the chest and are correctly proportioned, the value of the chest may not be greatly affected. This late 17th-century oak chest would be worth buying even with replaced bracket feet.
£1,000–1,500

ALTERATIONS

The size of a chest affects its value markedly. Small ones are particularly desirable, but sometimes larger chests are reduced in size to make them more valuable or convenient. On this example, which was made c.1710, note that the feet are oddly disproportionate. The marked difference in the depth of the two long drawers suggests that there may once have been another drawer. £1,200–1,800

▲ OYSTER VENEERING

Chests using carcasses of less expensive woods (usually oak or pine) and decorated with thin layers of attractively grained wood (a technique known as 'veneering') became popular in the late 17th century (see also p.44). This chest, which was made c.1695, has oyster veneers that are made by slicing smaller branches of wood like sausages. The veneer adds considerably to the value of this chest, and, even though it is in poor condition generally, it is worth £2,000 to £2,500. Properly restored, this chest could make in excess of £10,000.

STYLES OF FEET

Feet can help to date a chest.

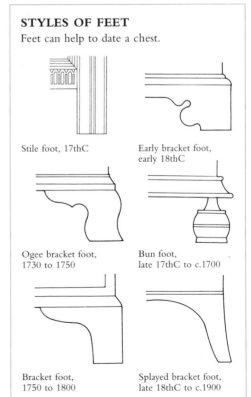

Stile foot, 17thC

Early bracket foot, early 18thC

Ogee bracket foot, 1730 to 1750

Bun foot, late 17thC to c.1700

Bracket foot, 1750 to 1800

Splayed bracket foot, late 18thC to c.1900

LATER CHESTS OF DRAWERS

Solid mahogany and mahogany veneer were used to make chests from c.1730 onwards. Quality and prices vary but features such as bow-fronts, brushing slides, canted (angled) corners, stringing and finely figured wood will all add to the value of a piece.

The most sought after chests are handsome 18th-century serpentine versions – they can cost £3,000 plus. Plainer mahogany chests, functional storage for bedrooms in the 18th,

19th and early 20th centuries, are just as useful today and good value at £400 to £800.

Today, among the most readily available chests of drawers are those dating from after c.1800, with pine or deal carcasses that are veneered with mahogany.

Chests that were constructed from pine, the least expensive of woods, can still be found in reasonable condition, painted or varnished, for as little as £250.

◀ VALUE
Flame mahogany-veneered drawer fronts add to the appeal of this serpentine mahogany chest made c.1770. Even though the stringing on the drawer fronts has been added at a later date, the chest would still be worth £2,500 to £3,000.

HOW OLD IS IT?

You may think that this walnut chest looks as though it was made in the 18th century, but a date of c.1930 would be more accurate for four main reasons:

● by the time serpentine chests became popular, from 1740 onwards, walnut was no longer fashionable;

● the veneer is machine-made;

● the distressing on the drawer fronts (shown left) is much too regular;

● the proportions of the chest – too tall with oversize bracket feet – are wrong.

THIS SOLID MAHOGANY CHEST MADE C.1760 APPEARS QUITE TALL AT 42 IN (107 CM), BUT IT IS THE CORRECT HEIGHT FOR A CHEST OF THIS PERIOD – MANY CHESTS HAVE BEEN CUT DOWN AT A LATER DATE. £1,000–1,500

The colour is deep and rich, but the chest has recently been over-varnished; this will tone down over time.

There are no extra holes inside the drawers and no marks caused by other handles outside, so these swan neck handles are original.

The drawers are pine-lined – a finer piece of this date would have oak linings, but after 1780 pine linings became increasingly common in chests.

These brasses have recently been cleaned and are very bright. If in doubt, it is better not to clean brasses, but if you like them to be shiny, cut a card template to fit round the handles to protect the wood before you polish them.

Drawers in the 17th, 18th and 19th centuries were always fitted with locks – these are made from good quality steel. A better quality chest of this date might have had brass locks.

The original bracket feet in such complete condition are a bonus – very often they have been cut down.

OTHER CHESTS OF DRAWERS

From the late 18th century onwards, the chest of drawers evolved into new, more specialized forms. Biedermeier chests were produced in Germany, Austria and Scandinavia from c.1820 to 1830. Made from pale-coloured woods, these chests have a strong architectural appearance, which has made them popular with interior decorators in recent years. Wellington chests are tall and narrow, usually with seven drawers. They became popular in England and France (where they were known as *semaniers* in the early 1800s). Campaign chests, originally designed for officers on army manoeuvres,

◄ BIEDERMEIER
This early Biedermeier birch chest of drawers has a rather strong architectural appearance with its chequered frieze and ebonized columns. Later and plainer pieces can be much less expensive. Beware – there are many modern imports on the market.
£2,000–3,000

▶ CAMPAIGN CHESTS
Campaign chests often contain hidden surprises. Some hold folding tables and a set of four chairs. This one, which was made c.1870 from solid teak, has a *secretaire* drawer that adds considerably to its value, even though the piece is in such battered condition overall.
£1,000–2,000

◄ PINE CHESTS
Pine was used to make chests for servants and poorer households from c.1750. Most old pine chests were originally scumble-painted (see p.158), although they are usually sold stripped nowadays. To find one (such as this one) with its original paint is a bonus – look out for a soft colour. Prices range from £150 to £400, but you should beware of reproductions (see also pp.156–57).

could be separated into two parts to be carried from camp to camp. Shaker chests were constructed from indigenous North American woods such as pine, maple, butternut and cherry. Some have large, flat tops and were used as work counters. Today, Shaker simplicity fits very well with modern interiors and is avidly sought. Prices can rocket to an amazing six figures for the very best pieces. For example, Oprah Winfrey paid an astounding £140,000 for the pine Shaker counter below. A tiger maple counter, considered to be one of the finest pieces of Shaker furniture, sold recently for £160,000.

◀ WELLINGTON CHESTS

Instead of each drawer having its own lock, English Wellington chests have an unusual single locking mechanism. The hinged flap on the right locks over the drawer fronts to stop them opening (see the detail above, right). The most valuable

Wellington chests are those with *secretaire* drawers; these are often contained in the second and third drawer fronts. £5,000–10,000

SHAKER FURNITURE

The Shakers were a self-sufficient religious community founded by Mother Ann Lee that flourished in the United States during the 19th century. They followed strict codes of behaviour and believed that the furniture they built should be as simple as possible in order to bring them closer to God. Simple, spare Shaker furniture, made for their own use and for sale to 'the world's people' (in other words, non-Shakers), has become highly fashionable and is still being made today.

▼ SHAKER COUNTER

This world-record-breaking Shaker counter is especially valuable because it has its original red paint and is marked by the craftsman who made it in 1830. Most Shaker chests cost £1,200 to £2,500, but you may have to go to the United States to find one.

CHESTS-ON-STANDS & CHESTS-ON-CHESTS

Chests-on-stands (known as 'highboys' in the United States) were popular in England from the 1660s to 1720s, when they were replaced by chests-on-chests (tallboys). Chests-on-stands are not as capacious as chests-on-chests but they are arguably more elegant. However, very few have survived with their original stands intact. They are often seen with replacement bun feet and no legs, giving them a rather odd, dumpy appearance.

▲ CHESTS-ON-CHESTS
Look out for chests-on-chests with concave inlaid sunbursts – a decorative feature that can multiply prices. This walnut *secretaire* tallboy, made c.1730, has a sunburst and the double bonus of a top drawer in the lower part that opens at 90°, enclosing small drawers and a writing surface. Even in poor condition this piece is still worth £5,000 to £7,000, and if restored could fetch up to £20,000.

▼ GRAINING
The attractive graining, showing the medullary (or star-like) rays, adds to the value of this late 17th-century solid oak chest-on-stand, as does the elaborate ogee (curving arch) apron. As with most pieces of this type, the chest has short drawers at the top and in the stand, and graduated long drawers in between.
£1,000–1,500

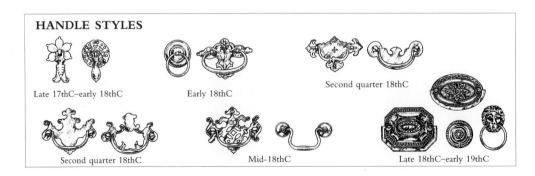

HANDLE STYLES

Late 17thC–early 18thC

Early 18thC

Second quarter 18thC

Second quarter 18thC

Mid-18thC

Late 18thC–early 19thC

THIS WALNUT-
VENEERED CHEST-ON-
CHEST MADE C.1720,
OF AVERAGE QUALITY
AND CONDITION, HAS
MANY REASSURING
SIGNS OF AGE AND
AUTHENTICITY THAT
YOU SHOULD LOOK
FOR IN EARLY
CASE FURNITURE.
£3,000–5,000

On 17th- and early
18th-century drawers,
the grain of the drawer
bottoms usually runs
from front to back, as
in the detail of a drawer
from this chest. After
c.1750 the grain usually
runs widthways (see
pp.42–43).

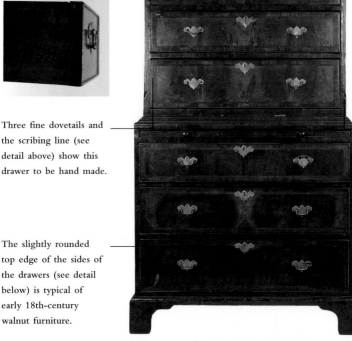

Three fine dovetails and
the scribing line (see
detail above) show this
drawer to be hand made.

The chipped area (see
detail above) shows that
the walnut veneer is thick
and often uneven – as it
will be if it has been
hand-cut.

The slightly rounded
top edge of the sides of
the drawers (see detail
below) is typical of
early 18th-century
walnut furniture.

The handles on this
piece are the right type
for the date but you can
see from inside (see
details below) that they
are replacements.

COMMODES

A commode is a grand chest, often of serpentine, semi-circular or *bombé* shape, incorporating either cupboards or drawers, or a combination of both. These, the most expensive and elaborate of chests, originated in France in the early 18th century (the word 'commode' means 'convenient' in French) and the design was first adapted in England by Thomas Chippendale in the mid-18th century.

Because they were very much luxury items made from the most costly materials, you are unlikely to find a 'bargain' commode today; even the cheapest are likely to fetch £3,000 to £4,000 at auction, while the most desirable can go for stellar prices.

THOMAS CHIPPENDALE (1718–1779)

Thomas Chippendale, the most influential furniture designer of his age, popularized rococo styles in England. In 1754, Chippendale published a famous book of designs called *The Gentleman and Cabinet-maker's Director.* It was printed in several editions and sold to cabinet-makers and wealthy patrons in England and North America, many of whom copied his designs. Chippendale did not sign his work, so only a few pieces of furniture can be definitely attributed.

▲ STAR QUALITY
Thought to be the work of émigré cabinet-maker, Pierre Langlois, this carved mahogany-veneered commode c.1770, reflecting the French rococo style, looks elaborate with its serpentine shape, gilt metal mounts and curving apron. However, if you compared it to earlier rococo examples made in France or by the English cabinet-maker, Thomas Chippendale, it would seem quite plain because there is no carved decoration. £30,000–50,000+

▶ **VALUE**

These two D-shaped commodes may look fairly similar, but the one above, made c.1780, is worth four times as much as the one below, which was made a century later, c.1890. Both are in the manner of George Seddon, a late 18th-century cabinet-maker renowned for painted satinwood furniture. Compare the painting and you will see the difference between the two: the flowers on the 18th-century commode (top) are fluid, while on the other the design is awkward.

Top £20,000–25,000
Bottom £5,000–7,000

BEWARE

Do not confuse these lavish pieces with what the Victorians also called 'commodes' – cupboards to hold their chamber pots! (Shown on p.144.)

◀ **FRENCH COMMODES**

French commodes, such as this one made in 1990 in the Louis XV style, usually have tops made from loose marble slabs. In England, marble was not used until the Victorian period, when copies of French commodes were often made with the marble tops held in place by metal galleries.

£5,000–8,000

Seating at one time reflected social status, and in the Middle Ages often only the head of a household had a chair, while everyone else sat on benches or stools. During the 17th century, chairs were made with upholstered seats, and some had spiral turnings or elaborate carving with scrolls and leaves. Most sets of dining chairs date from after 1700. Walnut dining chairs of the early 18th century are quite restrained in their use of carving and rely on their elegant shapes to make them pleasing to the eye. From the mid-18th century onwards fashions for seating were established by the designs engraved in the books of the leading furniture makers such as Thomas Chippendale, George Hepplewhite and Thomas Sheraton. Their designs were widely copied, and many were again reproduced in the late 19th and early 20th centuries.

Prices for chairs depend not only on quality but also on the number in the set. In the 18th century, dining chairs were commonly made in sets of 12 or 14, but these have often been split up. A set of eight or more dining chairs with two carvers is especially desirable. Each chair in a set will cost considerably more than one bought individually. One way of affording a set of chairs is to form a 'harlequin' set. Choose a common design and buy chairs individually or two or three pairs of similar chairs.

DINING CHAIRS

By their very nature, dining chairs are usually subjected to considerable wear and tear as they are sat on and moved around over the years. For this reason, it is important to take the condition of a set or individual chair into account before buying.

To test the strength of a chair, stand in front of it, gently put your knee on the seat and press the back – it should feel firm, with no 'give'. If you buy rickety chairs, have them re-glued before using them – falling through an unsafe chair might damage more than your pride!

▲ ARMCHAIRS
Armchairs from a set of dining chairs should be wider than the matching side chairs, as is the case with this one from a set of 14 made c.1770. Some side chairs have later arms added to make the set more valuable, so always compare widths of the seats of arm and side chairs, and be suspicious if they are the same – an original armchair should be up to 2in (5cm) wider.
£8,000–10,000
(for a set of 14)

WHICH ONE IS A COPY?

The stylish chair designs of the mid-18th century were much copied during the late 19th and early 20th centuries. There is nothing wrong with buying a copy, if you recognize it as such and as long as you are not paying over the odds for it. The chart below shows you the most important factors to look out for when purchasing.

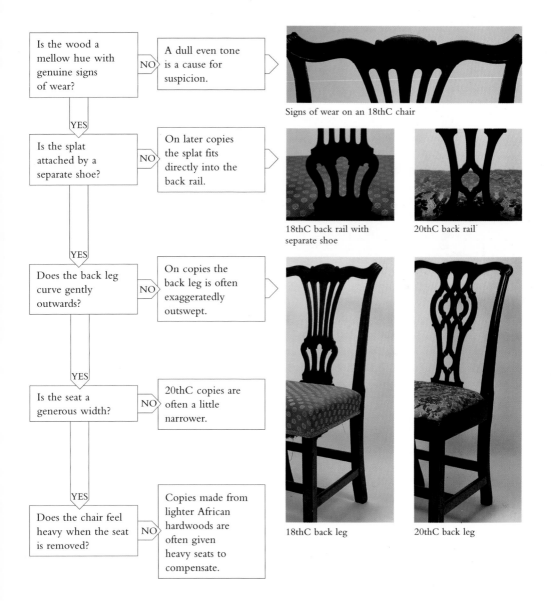

Is the wood a mellow hue with genuine signs of wear? — NO → A dull even tone is a cause for suspicion.

Signs of wear on an 18thC chair

YES

Is the splat attached by a separate shoe? — NO → On later copies the splat fits directly into the back rail.

18thC back rail with separate shoe

20thC back rail

YES

Does the back leg curve gently outwards? — NO → On copies the back leg is often exaggeratedly outswept.

YES

Is the seat a generous width? — NO → 20thC copies are often a little narrower.

YES

Does the chair feel heavy when the seat is removed? — NO → Copies made from lighter African hardwoods are often given heavy seats to compensate.

18thC back leg

20thC back leg

THE CHAIR ON THE LEFT, BASED ON A CHIPPENDALE DESIGN, DATES FROM c.1770. THE ONE ON THE RIGHT IS A GOOD QUALITY, EARLY 20TH-CENTURY COPY.

OTHER DINING CHAIRS

The designs of George Hepplewhite and Thomas Sheraton dominated the appearance of chairs in the last quarter of the 18th century. Hepplewhite's shield-back chair design was one of his most popular, while Sheraton introduced square-backed chairs of lighter proportions. Chair seats became narrower at the end of the 19th century, as the demand

	GEORGE III	EARLY 19TH CENTURY	MID-19TH CENTURY
	MAHOGANY DINING CHAIR c.1780	MAHOGANY DINING CHAIR c.1825	VICTORIAN SALON CHAIR c.1860
WHERE, WHEN, WHY	Decorative motifs drawn from Classical antiquity, such as the anthemion flower on the pierced back splat of this chair, are characteristic of chairs made in the third quarter of the 18th century in England, after designs by Hepplewhite.	Made between 1810 and 1840, the Regency to early Victorian period, a curved top-rail and the outswept back legs reflect the influence of ancient Greek seating. The seat is stuffed but not sprung.	Salon suites of six side chairs with matching settee and armchairs originated in Europe and were popular from c.1850 to 1910 in England. It is rare to find these in sets of more than six, or with arms.
WHAT TO LOOK FOR	● Detailed carving on the back splat – a sign of quality. ● Original stretchers. ● Drop-in seats – they are easier to re-upholster than the fitted variety.	● Circular tapering reeded legs, or outward curving sabre legs; chairs of lesser quality have simpler legs. ● Sets of six chairs with two matching armchairs.	● Balloon backs with cabriole legs more sought after than those with straight legs. ● Walnut and rosewood, followed by mahogany, are the most desirable woods; stained beech is considered less valuable.
PRICES	£150–200 each for single chairs. £4,000–5,000 for a set of six with two matching armchairs.	£2,000–3,000 for eight. £6,000 for six with two matching armchairs.	£800–1,200 for a set of six in mahogany with cabriole legs. £1,000–1,500 for eight with turned legs.

grew for chairs that would fit into smaller rooms. Mahogany remained the wood that was commonly used for formal dining chairs, but walnut and rosewood were also used to produce quality sets. While Gillow – leading 19th-century furniture makers – favoured oak, many less expensive chairs were made from stained beech.

ART NOUVEAU	EDWARDIAN	THONET CHAIRS	
STAINED BEECH CHAIR c.1900	MAHOGANY DINING CHAIR c.1900	BENTWOOD CHAIR c.1900	
Old decorative forms were interpreted in new ways in Art Nouveau chairs made in the early 20th century. Here, the form of turning and tapering and the elongated proportions are characteristically Art Nouveau.	In England the chair designs of Sheraton and Hepplewhite became fashionable again in the late 19th century. The proportions in later versions tend to be less generous, with thinner arms, legs and splats.	Michael Thonet was an innovative 19th-century German designer who developed a technique for mass-producing bentwood furniture. By 1900, he had factories throughout Europe and America that made over six million chairs from beech that had been steamed, bent and stained.	WHERE, WHEN, WHY
• Sculptural and unusual designs. • Chairs more akin to a design by a well-known designer e.g. Mackintosh, Voysey or Mackmurdo. • Original upholstery (although this does not always add value).	• Stringing, popular in the Edwardian era, but rare in 18th century, is found on better-quality chairs, often made of East Indian satinwood. • Reasonably sturdy proportions – some have spindly appearances.	• The original Thonet brand mark or label under the seat rim or that of the lesser-known maker, Kohn. • Good condition – these chairs are quite easy to find and, therefore, not worth buying if damaged.	WHAT TO LOOK FOR
£200–300 for the set of six beech chairs (above).	£1,500–2,000 for a set of eight with two armchairs.	£10–20 for a single chair.	PRICES

COUNTRY CHAIRS

Country chairs, many of which were made in remote rural areas, developed independently from the fashionable seating featured on the preceding pages.

Country chairs are always made of solid wood from indigenous trees: elm, yew, oak, ash and beech. The wood used can have a significant bearing on the price. Chairs made entirely or partly from yew are particularly sought after, while beech is more common. Dating can be a tricky business because designs changed little between the 18th and early 20th centuries, although examining the patina of the wood and the decorative details can be of considerable help.

If the chair combines decoration typical of different periods, always date it by the latest decorative detail.

▶ STYLES
Most country chairs vary more because of where, rather than when, they were made. The elaborately arched splats on this oak chair are typical of chairs made in South Yorkshire and Derbyshire, while the bobbin turning on the front stretcher dates the chair to the late 17th century.
£1,000–1,500

▼ SETS
The number of chairs in a set can affect the price dramatically. This simple ash and elm early 19th-century Windsor is from a set of five that would cost £600 to £900. If there were six chairs, the set would cost about £800 to £1,200; at the other end of the scale, you might find a single one for £100.

◀ LADDER BACKS
The six horizontal splats on this rush-seated early 19th-century ash armchair are responsible for its name: 'ladder back'. The rush seat looks a little sagged but could be restored without affecting the piece's value.
£250–350

EXAMINE A WINDSOR CLOSELY, AS THE COMBINATION OF WOODS CAN AFFECT VALUE. THIS ARMCHAIR, MADE FROM SOLID ASH AND ELM, IS WORTH £300 TO £400. IF IT INCLUDED YEW, IT WOULD BE MORE DESIRABLE AND COST £600 TO £900.

The higher and more elaborate the back, the more expensive the Windsor will be – this splat is fairly simple.

As with most country chairs you will find, this one has an elm saddle-shaped seat.

Check the splat, top rail and arms for cracks; you should be especially careful if they are made from yew, which is more brittle than ash.

The heavy turned legs date the chair to c.1825–50; an earlier chair would have cabriole legs. The turning on the back legs should match that on the front – if it does not, it could be a sign that some of the legs are replacements.

The crinoline stretcher, more commonly seen on 18th-century chairs, adds value.

HOW DID WINDSORS GET THEIR NAME?

According to one legend, George III, out riding near Windsor Castle, was caught in a storm and took refuge in a cottage. He took such a liking to the seat he rested on that they became known as 'Windsor' chairs. A more mundane explanation is that the chairs were originally made in the area surrounding Windsor.

CHAIR STYLES

Illustrated here are various designs dating from the late 17th century to the 1930s.

Early seating was very basic and limited to oak joined stools and settles. It was not until the 17th century that chairs were elaborately turned and carved. Some incorporated inlaid marquetry decoration.

Chairs of the Carolean period are usually of walnut, oak or stained beech, with caned seats, barley-twist supports and tall backs.

The cabriole leg dominated the early 18th century; by the 1750s, styles were being influenced by designs that could be found in the pattern books of Chippendale, Sheraton and Hepplewhite.

Sabre legs are associated with the Regency period, when chairs were usually mahogany or rosewood and of ornate design. French Empire styles continued to be an important influence (especially on chairs being made in America).

Victorian designs were sturdier and more ornate, while the Edwardians returned to the elegance of the late 18th century, although the chairs tended to be slightly narrower.

After the World War I, designers rediscovered the early 18th century, mixing Queen Anne and later Georgian or 'Chippendale' styles in an eclectic muddle.

Bobbin-turned, c.1640

Late 17thC York and Derbyshire

High-back Daniel Marot-style chair, c.1695

Queen Anne vase splat chair, c.1710

Ladder-back chair, mid-18thC

Intricately carved splat, c.1755

Provincial Chippendale, c.1770

Hepplewhite shield-back, c.1780

Serpentine top rail, c.1780

Sheraton, c.1795

Regency, c.1810

Early Victorian, c.1840

Sheraton Revival, c.1910

Chippendale Revival, early 20thC

Queen Anne Revival, c.1930

OPEN ARMCHAIRS

During the 18th century, the increasing importance attached to comfort and luxury led to the development of a wide range of sumptuously upholstered open armchairs. Although seats were generally stuffed rather than sprung, many had loose feather-filled cushions that made them very comfortable.

Armchair design was led by the French. Many English armchairs produced in the 18th and 19th centuries are based on French prototypes of the Louis XV and Louis XVI periods. Pairs are particularly sought after and will usually cost more than twice the price of a single constituent chair.

▶ WALNUT ARMCHAIRS
The shell that you can see at the top of the cabriole legs and on the centre of the back splat of this French walnut armchair, made about 1720, is one of the most popular motifs to be found on early 18th-century furniture. This piece is worth £3,000 to £5,000.

▲ FRENCH OR ENGLISH?
When it comes to mid-19th-century furniture, deciding whether a piece is English or French can be difficult. The chair on the left, in the Louis XV style, was made by the popular English makers Howard & Sons in the 1860s. The construction of the Louis XVI-style chair on the right suggests that it was made in France, but in fact it carries a Howard & Sons' label, probably because it was retailed or repaired by them.
£800–1,200 (left)
£700–1,000 (right)

► **BUTLERS' CHAIRS**
Although the seat
is not upholstered,
this interesting, late
19th-century oak chair,
with original buttoned
moquette upholstery, is
very comfortable. The
chair was probably
made for the sitting-
room of a head butler
in a grand house; today
it would be equally
practical for sitting at
a desk.
£200–300

▼ **WHAT'S IN
A NAME?**
Chairs made by leading
manufacturers in the
19th century were
occasionally marked
with their names.
If you can find the
manufacturer's stamp (it
is often under the seat
rail or inside the back
leg), it can dramatically
increase the value of
the chair. Although this
walnut armchair, made
about 1865, is battered
and worn, it would be
worth buying and
restoring because it is
stamped by Gillow,
leading makers of the
period.
£2,000–3,000
(in this condition)
£3,000–4,000
(restored)

NAMES TO LOOK OUT FOR
Gillow (Lancaster)
Howard & Sons (London)
Krieger (Paris) (stamped on the arm)
Lexcellent (Paris)
Maple (London)
Thomas Schoolbred (London)

▲ **CASTERS**
French chairs often
had wooden casters so
that they would not
scratch wooden floors.
In England, where
carpets were generally
favoured, casters in the
18th century were
often made from brass
with leather-bound
wheels (as in the detail,
left). Later, in the 18th
century, they were
just brass wheels.
Some were stamped
by their makers
(Cope & Collinson
are particularly well
known). In the 19th
century, less expensive
chairs were made with
ceramic casters, which
are of less interest to
collectors. Note: you
should never remove
the old casters from a
chair, as this will reduce
its value.

BERGÈRES & WING ARMCHAIRS

In France, during the reign of Louis XV (1715–1774), a greater emphasis on comfort and display led to the development, c.1725, of the bergère: an armchair (although some versions have open arms) with a concave back and solid upholstered sides.

Bergères must have been very welcome in the large draughty salons of the 18th century, with their sumptuously filled, deep feather cushions. French 18th-century versions were very much a rich person's seat, and they are still relatively expensive today.

Bergères made in England during the mid-19th century tend to be more affordable, if less luxurious. American bergère-type easy chairs, c.1820–40, have rounded top rails of wood that continue down the arms to form the hand holds.

► **FRENCH BERGÈRES**
Caning, used on the sides of this Louis XVI beechwood bergère, was popular on French furniture throughout the 18th century, but not as commonly used in England until c.1800. French chair frames were always made of beech, either left plain, as here, or gilded or painted.
£1,500–2,000

◄ **WING ARMCHAIRS**
The generously shaped wings on this c.1780 armchair add to its value, even though the simple mahogany frame with low stretcher shows that it is of provincial origin.
£1,500–2,000

RE-UPHOLSTERING
Always choose a good-quality fabric that is appropriate to the date and style of a chair, and take the cost of re-upholstering into account before you buy a chair in obviously poor condition. Re-upholstering can be an expensive process that more than doubles the cost of the chair.

► **ENGLISH BERGÈRES**
The concave back on this c.1830 mahogany bergère is inspired by the Klismos chairs of ancient Greece. Although 19th-century bergères tend to vary in quality, you can tell that this is a good example by the deep gadrooning (the fluted decoration) and the patera (classical flower heads) on the legs.
£1,000–1,500

◄ **EASY CHAIRS**
This easy chair, made by Howard & Sons c.1870, would present its buyer with a dilemma: the upholstery, a Voysey-style fabric from c.1900, is not original, although it is very interesting in its own right.
£1,000–1,500

BEWARE
Do not put springs in an 18th-century chair that originally had a stuffed seat.

MISCELLANEOUS CHAIRS

The huge range of chairs that is sold – in pairs or individually – offers a golden opportunity to find affordable seating of almost any date and style that you care to imagine. Some of the miscellaneous chairs that you will find, such as the high-back oak chair (right), may once have been part of a larger set, but by buying a single chair you will pay less than half the price of a chair in a set. As with any chair, be sure to sit on it *before* buying it; you should make certain that it is both comfortable and sturdy.

◀ OAK HIGH-BACK
Daniel Marot, a French Huguenot émigré, designed heavily carved oak chairs such as this one in the late 17th century. The style became popular again in the late 19th and early 20th centuries, when vast numbers of chairs were made in factory workshops in Malines, Belgium.
£50–100 (for one)
£1,500–1,800 (for a set of eight)

▼ OVAL-BACK CHAIRS
This elegantly simple mahogany chair with a stuffed oval back, made c.1780, was probably once part of a larger set used in the dining-room. Chairs of this type often have spring-upholstered seats that have been added by Victorian upholsterers.
£300–500

▲ HALL CHAIRS
Decorative, but not very comfortable, hall chairs are the seats on which you would have waited for an audience with the master of the household. Nowadays, it is far more common to see hall chairs used as low tables beside sofas. This is a rather superior example, made about 1815 from solid mahogany. It has been stamped by its maker: P. Hill.
£400–600

▼ GONDOLA CHAIRS

The Regency fondness for Greek forms is reflected in the design of this beech gondola chair made c.1810. Chairs such as this one were often ebonized and later stripped. This piece would sell for £1,000 to £1,500.

▼ CLUB ARMCHAIRS

Made for gentlemen's clubs, chairs such as this mahogany example, made c.1830, were also produced in oak or rosewood. A chair of this date would not originally have had casters; the ones on this chair are Victorian additions. £800–1,200

▶ SWISS CHAIRS

Visitors to Switzerland in the 19th century often brought back these chairs with rusticated legs as souvenirs. This one has an adjustable seat and could be used as a piano chair. £400–600

▶ ROCKERS

Large numbers of rockers were made in America during the 19th century by firms such as George Hinzinger, often in the Eastlake taste: a practical and simplified Gothic Reform style. On this example, made between 1880 and 1900, the beechwood has been attractively carved to simulate bamboo – this is a definite plus. £80–120

EARLY SETTEES & SOFAS

What is the difference between a sofa and a settee? The distinction is a fuzzy one, but the word 'settee' was derived from 'settle', the earliest form of seating for two or more people. The word 'sofa' is of Middle Eastern derivation (denoting the 'dais' on which the Grand Vizier sat) and did not appear in England until the 18th century. Nowadays, however, the two terms often overlap, although the word 'sofa' usually refers to a seat that is both larger and more comfortable than a settee.

◀ SETTLES

Settles are the forerunners of settees, and their tall backs are similar to those of chairs of the same date. This one is of simple panelled construction and dates from c.1710. It is worth noting that a settee of the same date would have a similar high back. £1,000–1,500

STYLES

Other popular settee designs from the 18th and 19th centuries:

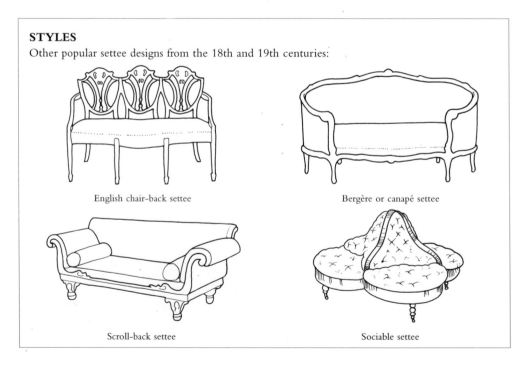

English chair-back settee

Bergère or canapé settee

Scroll-back settee

Sociable settee

◀ SETTEE BACKS
Perhaps in order to
protect expensive
upholstery from the
fashionable powdered
wigs of the 18th
century, the backs of
sofas, such as this one
made c.1730, became
lower. On this example
the arched back gives a
softer line. In France,
the undulating backs of
sofas were sometimes
designed to fit into the
moulding of similarly
curved wall panelling.
£8,000–12,000

▶ FRENCH SETTEES
The *Duchesse* is a type
of *chaise longue* that
became popular in
France during the reign
of Louis XV. This one
is called a *Duchesse
brisée*, as it is 'broken'
in two sections; others
come in three sections
with stools. Copies
were made in large
numbers c.1900.
£2,000–3,000

**◀ PAINTED
SETTEES**
Painted furniture was
very fashionable in
the late 18th century.
This pastel-painted,
neo-classical-style
sofa, made c.1780,
has an elaborate camel
back and a double
serpentine seat rail that
add to its value.
£3,000–5,000

LATER SETTEES & SOFAS

An important development changed the appearance of many sofas made after 1830. Earlier sofas were stuffed with layers of horsehair and wadding; spring upholstered sofas, introduced from c.1830, had seats and backs filled with metal springs that were supported on hessian webbing and then covered in layers of horsehair and wadding. In order to make room for the new springs, sofas became deeper and wider, and buttoning was often used to make them look even more sumptuous.

▶ **BIEDERMEIER SOFAS**
Plain German and Scandinavian Biedermeier sofas, made c.1825 from inexpensive mahogany veneer, are often modestly priced. Extra architectural details, however, can increase the price dramatically.
£800–1,200

INSIDE A SPRUNG SOFA
From 1830 onwards, most sofas were upholstered with coiled metal springs covered with padding and webbing, making them far more comfortable.

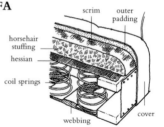

◀ *CHAISES LONGUES* **OR** *RECAMIERS*
Often made in mirror image pairs (with the head rests at opposite ends), *chaises longues*, such as this rosewood example made c.1840, are now usually sold singly. Their elegance ensures that they are still in keen demand.
£1,000–1,500

SALON SUITES, COMPRISING A SETTEE, AN OPEN ARMCHAIR (CALLED A 'GRANDFATHER') AND A LOW CHAIR (CALLED A 'GRANDMOTHER'), WERE MADE FROM C.1840 ONWARDS. SOME SUITES ALSO HAD MATCHING SIDE CHAIRS. GOOD EARLY SUITES ARE NOT EASY TO FIND COMPLETE BUT THEY USUALLY REPRESENT GOOD VALUE, OFTEN COSTING LESS THAN A GOOD-QUALITY MODERN EQUIVALENT. THIS ONE INCLUDES SIX PIECES (SETTEE, THREE CHAIRS AND TWO STOOLS) AND WOULD BE WORTH £2,500 TO £4,000.

The frame is walnut but it could equally have been rosewood or mahogany.

The pierced back looks elegant but it probably acted as a chaperone for amorous couples!

Buttoning was very popular at this date and often covers the entire back and seats of settees.

The cabriole leg indicates that the suite dates from the earlier part of Queen Victoria's reign, c.1850; later suites have turned legs.

The stool is a good match but it does not belong to the original suite.

LATER SUITES

This 1880s chair from a salon suite is of much lower quality than the pieces above. This means, however, that it would be less expensive and easier to find. A seven-piece suite would fetch £700 to 1,000; this chair is worth £100.

STOOLS

A status symbol, an extravagant accessory, a seat, and something to put your feet on – the humble stool has played a multitude of roles since it first appeared in ancient times. At medieval court the stool showed rank – only honoured guests could use them – the king sat on a throne, everyone else stood.

Among the most elegant and expensive stools are those inspired by antiquity. Robert Adam designed a stool modelled on a Roman cistern (a water tank), and the X-form stool, used by Ancient Egyptians, Romans and Greeks, became enormously popular in the Regency period (the Ancient Egyptians made a wide range of stools in materials ranging from papyrus and wicker to wood and ivory).

American stools often reflect European designs. The joint stool, for example, which was usually made of oak, was produced from the 17th century onwards in both continents.

A good 18th-century or Regency stool might cost several thousand pounds, but you can often find 19th- and 20th-century pieces for about £100.

◀ 18TH-CENTURY STOOLS
You can tell from its deep sides that this simple walnut stool, made c.1730, was once a commode (the sides hid the chamber pot). The 18th-century crewelwork covering is a plus, even though it is not original to the stool.
£800–1,200

HOW OLD ARE THEY?

The earliest form of stool commonly seen today, the joint stool, was first popular in the 17th century (far left); it was also reproduced in large numbers in the 1930s (left). There are a number of signs of age that you should look for, including:
● a mellow sheen with variations in tone where the stool has been exposed to wear;
● genuine wear on the stretchers – here, the modern version's stretchers are artificially worn in the centre;
● irregular-shaped pegs that stand proud; but beware – copies have machine-cut pegs that are sometimes left proud to give an impression of shrinkage;
● a dry appearance underneath.

◄ X-FORM STOOLS
X-form stools, popular in the late 18th century, are often of superior quality and therefore expensive. This is one of a characteristically refined pair, made c.1800, with dished mahogany seats and elegant scrolled ends; a pair would be worth £3,000 to £4,000.

▲ PIANO STOOLS
Piano stools were first seen in the late 18th century; this rosewood example can be dated to c.1835 by its heavy proportions and the scrolling, rococo-style carving on its legs. £200–300

▲ MOORISH STOOLS
Large quantities of Moorish-style furniture were made throughout the Middle East (and especially in Cairo) for export to the West during the late 19th century. Most pieces feature elaborate turning, derived from Musharabyeh panelling (which is used for Oriental screens). This stool is made from stained softwood and would be relatively inexpensive; look out for walnut versions, which can be worth four times as much. £100–200

▲ POUFFES
The home-worked top of this horsehair-stuffed pouffe was probably made by a middle-class lady in the 1870s. Pouffes are among the least expensive stools available; this one might cost you £200.

Tables are still essential pieces of furniture and it is no surprise that they are second only to chairs in popularity with collectors.

During the 17th century the oak stretcher table was the most common type of dining table, but, from c.1700, both large and small tables became more varied in form. Ingenious extending tables were made by Regency cabinet-makers, and Victorian manufacturers quickly capitalized on these earlier inventive designs.

Comfort is, of course, an important consideration when you are choosing a dining table, so always try sitting at a few before you make your choice. Most are a standard 29in (74cm) high. If the table is much lower, it may have been reduced and will prove uncomfortable.

If the apron (the band that supports the top) is deep, the table may be awkward for a tall person to sit at – especially if the overhang of the top is skimpy.

Many of the classic tables that were designed in the 18th and early 19th centuries are still being reproduced today. A copy made, say, a few decades ago, which has been subjected to some wear, can mislead inexperienced collectors. If in doubt, you should compare the proportions and colour with one that you know to be genuine. Reproduction tables tend to be smaller and lighter, and the patina of the wood lacks the depth and richness that you would expect in the genuine article.

REFECTORY TABLES

The term 'refectory table' was recently coined to describe the long joined tables that were popular from c.1550 to 1700. This (along with the trestle table) is the earliest form of dining table. Some have huge single plank tops, but most have two or three pieces of wood cleated together. Stretcher tables are usually made from oak, although you can see tables that are made from elm or a combination of the two.

AS WITH MANY REFECTORY TABLES, THIS ONE, MADE c.1630, HAS HAD SOME ALTERATIONS AND REPAIRS. EVEN SO, IT IS AN ATTRACTIVE, GOOD-SIZED EXAMPLE, MEASURING 9 FT 6 IN (291 CM) IN LENGTH. IT IS WORTH £4,000 TO £6,000.

Spurious dates are often carved onto friezes but the carving on this piece is all original. It covers only one side because these tables were kept pushed against walls.

If the legs are quite thin, they might have been replaced. Heavy, bulbous legs are a preferable shape.

BEWARE

Large numbers of copies were produced at the turn of the 19th century, often made from oak floorboards. Check table tops for filled holes at even spaces – this could mean that the planks were originally nailed to joists as part of someone's floor! Also, check the difference in colour between the underside of the top and the inside of the skirt.

▶ WORN FEET

The feet on this Restoration table (made c.1660) have almost completely worn away. Originally, the stretcher would have been several inches off the ground, so that people could avoid the cold stone floor by resting their feet on it.
£8,000–12,000

The top is made from two planks and has the rich patination that you would expect to find on a period table.

The hard, square edges on the feet suggest that they are replacements.

These attractively shaped brackets are a sign of quality.

The joints should be pegged with dowels that stand slightly proud, owing to the gradual drying out and shrinkage of the wood. In this case, they have been replaced with screws.

◀ PERIOD

This table dates from the first quarter of the 17th century, making it a very desirable piece.
£4,000–6,000

GATELEG & DROP-LEAF TABLES

Ideal for less formal occasions or smaller houses, gateleg tables were first fashionable in the middle of the 17th century; some early versions had a leg halved vertically to form a support. The standard gateleg table has four fixed legs that are connected by stretchers, and pull-out gates that extend to support the flaps on either side. Larger tables sometimes have two pull-out gates on each side.

The drop-leaf table is an early 18th-century refinement of the gateleg and has four legs:

two fixed to opposite corners of the central panel and two that hinged out to support the two side flaps. By the mid-19th century, a much smaller version with deep rectangular flaps – known as a 'Sutherland' table – had become popular.

Most drop-leaf and gateleg tables are large enough to seat no more than six people comfortably, and, for this reason, they have remained among the most desirable early tables suitable for dining.

◀ SIZE
This 18th-century table is larger than most, measuring 6 ft 4 in (194 cm) at the widest point of its oval top. You could comfortably seat between 10 and 12 people at the table, for this reason it is worth £10,000 to £15,000. Six-seater gatelegs are more common and cost £1,000 to £2,000.

▶ COPIES
This is a reproduction gateleg table made c.1930. Giveaway signs include:
● the top and the stretchers are too thin;
● a high contrast in the grain on the top but no depth to the patina;
● the top edge has been moulded – earlier gatelegs had square-cut edges.
£200–300

WHAT TO LOOK FOR

Check the flaps and hinges for damage.
The hinges might be made from wooden
rule joints or from metal. The flaps (on
both gatelegs and drop-leaves) are quite
heavy and it is easy for the hinges to break,
causing the flaps to drop and split.

WOODS

● Always solid rather than veneered.
● The grain of the wood on the flaps and
the centre should run parallel to the hinges.
● Oak or oak and elm are usual for early
gatelegs.
● 18th-century drop-leaf tables are usually
mahogany.
● Country drop-leaves are found in oak,
elm or fruitwood.

▶ DROP-LEAF

As with most drop-
leaves, this one is made
from mahogany,
although you can also
find them made from
walnut. With its
elaborate claw and ball
feet it is surprising that
the maker has not made
cabriole legs (these are
turned). Even so, it
is an attractive table,
larger than most (with
six legs rather than
four) and good value
at £1,500 to £2,000.

◀ DESIGN

This drop-leaf table,
made from mahogany
c.1740, reveals the
practical advantage
of the design: it could
be put away when not
in use. The elegant
cabriole legs and simple
pad feet are typical of
this style of table.
£1,000–1,500

BREAKFAST & PEDESTAL TABLES

Pedestal or pillar dining tables were featured in the late 18th-century pattern books of Hepplewhite and Sheraton, although they had become less fashionable by the 1820s, by which time multi-legged tables were favoured (see p.90).

At the beginning of the Edwardian period in the early 20th century, as more and more large houses were divided into smaller living areas, the demand for large dining tables diminished; in response to this trend, dealers often rounded the corners of sections from large pedestal tables to make them into two or more breakfast tables.

Unfortunately, this widespread practice is not reversible, so there is a relative scarcity of good 18th- and 19th-century pillar dining tables – and an abundance of breakfast tables.

◀ PILLARS
Original 18th- or early 19th-century tables with three or more pillars are rare. This three-pillar version, made c.1800, has two extra leaves and could seat up to 14 people comfortably at full extension; it would, however, cost you £12,000 to £18,000. A two-pillar table of similar date would fetch £3,000 to £5,000.

◀ DECORATION
The edge of this table is crossbanded in rosewood, with an inlaid border of boxwood. Original 18th-century tables rarely have crossbanding, so this may be a reproduction, or the top a later embellishment.

▼ BREAKFAST TABLES
This photograph of a Regency mahogany table, made c.1810, shows the under-frame that allows the table top to tip and be pushed out of the way when it is not in use.
£1,500–2,000

WHAT TO LOOK FOR

Look under the top to make sure that there are plenty of finger stains around the edge of the table – this is a sign that the breakfast table has not been made from a cut-down dining table.

▼ **LATER PEDESTAL TABLES**
This late, good-quality table typifies the most up-to-date style of its time. It has a narrow apron, popular in the 1820s, and heavy downswept legs.
£8,000–12,000

BEWARE

Both pedestal dining tables and breakfast tables are copied today, often to a very high standard. Reproductions, such as this copy of a Victorian marquetry breakfast table, made c.1970, tend to be smaller, with thinner tops and legs, and do not have the depth of patina that you would see in a period example. This copy would fetch £1,750 to £2,500, the original would be worth £8,000 to £12,000.

LATER DINING TABLES

A variety of new and ingenious extending dining tables emerged in the early 19th century. The Cumberland action table stored the extra leaves and legs within a deep apron under the top. Robert Jupe, the innovative furniture maker, patented a capstan (rotating) circular extending table in 1836; when the top was twisted the segmented top opened, allowing the extra pieces to slot in. Other dining tables were extended with winding handles and telescopic sliders.

Prices for the best designs have rocketed in recent years. Circular tables have become especially fashionable, but you can still find some large and less spectacular Victorian tables for about £1,000. The elaborateness of the supports can affect price; the best have heavily carved pedestals or legs.

▶ CIRCULAR TABLES
This extending table dates from about 1880. The small supports pull out to hold segmented leaves around the edge. Missing these leaves it is worth £1,500 to £2,000; with them it would fetch between £5,000 and £8,000.

◀ RECTANGULAR TABLES
The two end sections of this Regency table pull open on a box frame to allow extra leaves to be inserted. Made c.1820, the table still has its original leaves and would fetch £4,000 to £6,000.

WOODS
Most 19th-century dining tables have tops made from solid mahogany, some with veneered friezes; solid oak was a less common alternative. Veneered tops are often found on reproduction tables.

WHAT TO LOOK FOR
● Make sure that the opening mechanism works well.
● Check that the legs are sturdy.
● Look for a well-figured top – this increases desirability.
● Elegant legs, such as the reeded ones on the table above, add visual appeal.

▶ **SPLIT-PILLAR TABLES**

The central pillar of this table splits in two and can hold three extra leaves. The grand C-scroll legs are typical of the rococo revival style of c.1840; similar tables were made in north Germany.
£6,000–8,000

◀ **VALUE**

While superior designs have risen dramatically in value, prices for less exceptional examples have remained steady. Made c.1860, this table extends with a winding handle to take three extra leaves; it measures 9ft 10in (3m) and seats 12 comfortably.
£2,000–3,000.

▲ **CRÈME DE LA CRÈME**

Extending tables made by the cabinet-maker Robert Jupe have attracted top prices recently. Only a decade ago they sold for £2,000 to £3,000, they change hands now for between £70,000 and £80,000. This William IV version, made c.1835, recently sold for £78,000.

LEGS & FEET STYLES

The variety of legs and feet found on tables, chairs and other furniture can help to date a piece. However, many styles were revived and reproduced in later periods; the style of a leg, therefore, is no guarantee of age and you should also take into account the appearance of the wood when dating.

Feet on caned furniture are frequently replaced, as damp floors often caused them to rot. Replacement feet will not necessarily reduce the value of a piece dramatically if their style is consistent with the date of that piece. Replacement legs, however, especially if they have all been replaced, should be viewed with more scepticism.

Having casters that are original to a piece is always desirable, especially if they are attached to decoratively carved feet.

Cup and cover,
1560–1680

Bobbin turned,
2nd half 17thC

Ball-turned,
2nd half 17thC

Barley twist,
1660–1710

Walnut scroll,
c.1675

Slender baluster,
1660–1800

Inverted cup baluster,
c.1675–1700

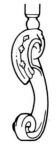

Carved scroll,
late 17thC

Queen Anne
cabriole leg,
early 18thC

Queen Anne
cabriole leg,
early 18thC

Claw and ball
foot, 1730–1750

Plain hoof foot,
c.1720

Plain club foot,
mid-18thC

Cabriole,
late 18thC French

Plain straight,
mid-18thC

Blind fretted,
mid-18thC

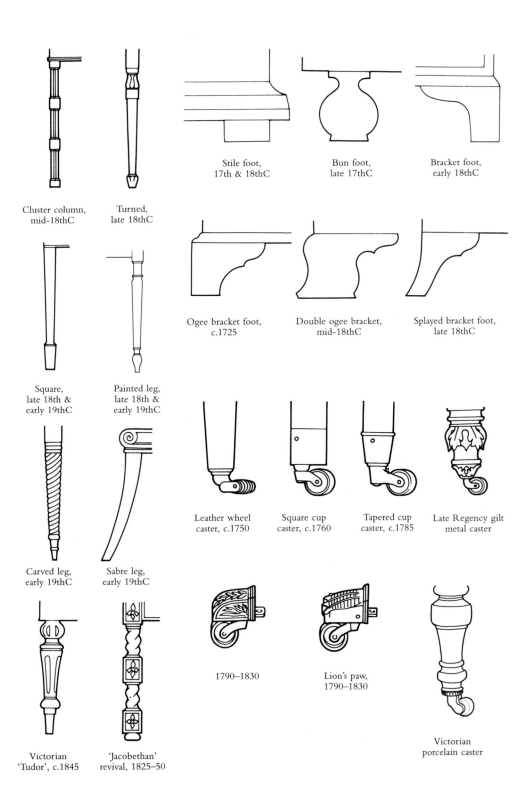

Cluster column,
mid-18thC

Turned,
late 18thC

Stile foot,
17th & 18thC

Bun foot,
late 17thC

Bracket foot,
early 18thC

Ogee bracket foot,
c.1725

Double ogee bracket,
mid-18thC

Splayed bracket foot,
late 18thC

Square,
late 18th &
early 19thC

Painted leg,
late 18th &
early 19thC

Leather wheel
caster, c.1750

Square cup
caster, c.1760

Tapered cup
caster, c.1785

Late Regency gilt
metal caster

Carved leg,
early 19thC

Sabre leg,
early 19thC

1790–1830

Lion's paw,
1790–1830

Victorian
'Tudor', c.1845

'Jacobethan'
revival, 1825–50

Victorian
porcelain caster

MEDIUM-SIZED TABLES

The Pembroke table, the forebear of the sofa table, was introduced in the mid-18th century. It was named after the Countess of Pembroke, who supposedly ordered the first one. Pembrokes have rectangular, circular, serpentine or oval tops, with flaps supported on small, hinged members called 'flys'.

The term 'Pembroke' table was used interchangeably with 'breakfast' table. They were used for light meals – breakfast and tea – or as work tables. The sofa table, which was a longer, narrower version of the Pembroke,

was designed to stand in front of a sofa and was used by ladies for writing, drawing and reading. The first ones appeared in the 1790s and were made of mahogany. Various exotic woods were also used for creating veneers. Marquetry decoration of neo-classical design is found on finer pieces.

Centre tables are similar in form to sofa tables, but they do not have the flaps at each end. Library tables tend to be very grand and expensive – the most elaborate versions have hinged tops for showing maps and prints.

▶ **PEMBROKE TABLES**
Sheraton-style Pembroke tables were widely copied in the late 19th and early 20th centuries. If you think that you have found one, examine the thickness of the veneers – later reproductions are covered in thin, machine-cut wood. This one is genuine: it was made c.1790 from mahogany and has satinwood banding – it is worth £1,200 to £1,800; later copies fetch £300 to £500.

◀ **SOFA TABLES**
The position of the stretcher on a sofa or centre table can give an indication of the table's date. The high stretcher on this painted satinwood table points to an early date of c.1790. A decade later stretchers were lower or had been replaced by central pedestals. Note the low stretcher on the library table opposite. £3,000–4,000

► **LIBRARY TABLES**
Library tables such as this one,
made c.1850 of walnut, usually
have leather tops. This one
reflects the eclectic Victorian
style: it mixes rococo C-scrolls
and Elizabethan motifs.
£2,000–3,000

◄ **PROVENANCE**
An illustrious provenance will
always boost the price of any
furniture. This well-worn
Victorian oak centre or library
table would normally sell for
£3,000 to £5,000. However,
because it was sold in a well-
publicized house sale at Stokesay
Court, Shropshire, it made more
than double the top estimate,
selling for nearly £6,500.

► **CONTINENTAL TABLES**
This Spanish kingwood veneered
centre table, made c.1860, is
similar to contemporary French
tables. Restrained though heavy,
it is clearly of high quality.
£2,000–3,000.

WORK TABLES

Ingeniously made small work tables, designed for ladies to store their sewing materials in, date from the late 18th century onwards and can vary considerably in form. The majority have silk bags underneath that pull out; some have hinged lids that open to reveal interiors fitted for sewing materials; others have hinged flap tops and pull-out slides. Thomas Sheraton, the 18th-century cabinet-maker, even designed one with a retractable fire-screen.

WHAT TO LOOK FOR

Because they are small, work tables were often veneered in the most expensive woods of the day. Look out for beautifully figured woods, such as the burr walnut one above, made c.1860, or exotic timbers such as coromandel, satinwood or kingwood. £500–800

▲ SHERATON-STYLE
This oval painted satinwood work table imitates the Sheraton-style furniture of the 1790s, even though it was made a century later, c.1890. One clue to the later date is the painting on the top of children playing – this is a typically nostalgic Victorian subject. £1,000–1,500

◀ RESTORATION
Replacement legs and handles will reduce value, but replacement bags often prove quite acceptable – provided that they are made from suitable materials. This run-of-the-mill mahogany table, made c.1830, has a well-made replacement bag in an appropriate fabric. £500–800

TRIPOD TABLES

Three-legged tables used for tea or dessert were the most popular small table of the 18th century. Most tripod tables have tops that can tip up into a vertical position when not in use. The least expensive versions, those with plain circular tops, can cost as little as £300 to £400, while finer examples are worth between £3,000 and £4,000.

The classic 18th-century tripod table has a top that is made from a single piece of solid mahogany (note that some American walnut tables have two-piece tops). Country tripod tables were made from oak, fruitwood and elm; some were decorated with parquetry veneers and there are others were even made from papier-mâché.

▲ COMPARISON

Both these tables were made c.1750 from solid mahogany. The table on the left is about six times more valuable, at £4000 to £6000, than the one on the right, and it has three decorative details that show its quality:

- the pie-crust top and its elaborately shaped edge;
- the fluted and leaf-carved baluster (most tables have only simple turned decoration);
- the hairy paw feet (simple pad feet are more common).

The table on the right appears to be the more elaborate of the two, but it is worth only £600 to £800. The price reflects the fact that it was once a plain tripod table, only more recently an elaborate supper table (probably c.1860 to 1880).

The tell-tale signs are:
- the carving is incised into the leg (as shown above), making it narrower; it should stand proud as it does on the table above left;
- the bearers were not cut down after the top was restyled, as a result they stick out;
- a lack of 'movement' in the carving of the leaves and foliage.

CONSTRUCTION

The top of the tripod table (above, left) is attached to the base by a birdcage support that allows the top to swivel, tip, or be removed.

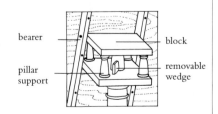

bearer

pillar support

block

removable wedge

CARD & GAMES TABLES

Fortunes were won and lost at cards in the 18th century and, from c.1690 onwards, numerous tables were produced especially for card-playing. As backgammon, chess and tric trac (a variation on backgammon) became popular, tables were made to accommodate these different games.

Tric trac tables often resemble Pembroke or sofa tables but for their removable panels:

these panels conceal wells that are divided in two. Prices for card and games tables reflect the demand for all small tables that fit well in modern sitting-rooms. Various woods were used, as well as papier-mâché.

A high-quality 18th-century concertina action table will fetch over £40,000. Less spectacular pieces, such as the ones shown below, are in the £500 to £12,000 range.

▼ **CONDITION**
The walnut veneer on this card table, made c.1710, is starved of colour; note also that the top has

warped, probably because it has been over-exposed to sunlight. Nevertheless, the fact that it opens in a highly elaborate way,

known as a 'concertina action' (see detail below), means that it would still be worth around £8,000 to £12,000.

▼ **DEMI-LUNE**
The D-shape or 'demi-lune' is a common shape for card tables and was particularly popular c.1780 (when this one was made). This table is slightly superior to most – both back legs open in a double gateleg action.
£800–1,200

CONCERTINA ACTION
The back legs of the table, attached to a hinged frieze, pull out to support the top when it is unfolded (as shown in this detail).

► **STYLE**

With its serpentine top and cabriole legs, this card table, made c.1770, was inspired by French designs of the 1750s. An English furniture maker, John Cobb, is often associated with this elegant style. £2,500–3,500

► **LATER CARD TABLES**

By the early 19th century card tables with central supports (and no legs to disturb the players) had become popular; today they are relatively inexpensive. The reeded baluster support on this swivel-top rosewood table, made c.1830, is typical of furniture made in the reign of William IV. £1,200–1,800

▼ **PAPIER-MÂCHÉ TABLES**

This papier-mâché chess and writing table, made c.1840, would originally have had an upper part with shelves and drawers that had to be removed before the inlaid mother-of-pearl chess board could be used. Because the top is missing, this piece is worth £500 to £800; with its top, it would fetch twice as much.

PAPIER-MÂCHÉ

Made from sheets of wet paper that were pasted together and pressed in moulds, a great deal of papier-mâché furniture was manufactured in the Birmingham area between 1820 and 1870. Once dried, the furniture was coated with layers of (usually) black lacquer and then decorated with gilt, painted decoration and thin slivers of mother-of-pearl.

The manufacturers Jennens & Bettridge are particularly associated with papier-mâché furniture; the appearance of their stamp on a piece will add some value.

OTHER SMALL TABLES I

Small tables tended to be simply made from solid wood until the late 17th century. Over the next two hundred years, as society became more sophisticated and interiors more refined, cabinet-makers produced an enormous variety of smaller tables, adorning them in a myriad ways: carving, gilding, marquetry, metal mounts and porcelain plaques are just some of the decorations that you will find on small tables made during the 18th, 19th and 20th centuries. Condition, ease of use (in other words, how practical they are in today's homes) and appearance are important factors in determining the value of all kinds of small table. Those made in the 18th century are often very elaborate and were produced for the wealthiest homes.

Many types of small table were used for serving tea or coffee, which were then seen as expensive commodities that deserved to be presented on a suitably extravagant stage. Console and pier tables were decorative

	SIDE TABLES	LOWBOY SIDE TABLES
	OAK SIDE TABLE c.1660–80 £1,000–1,500	OAK LOWBOY c.1740 £1,800–2,800
HOW, WHEN, WHY	The forerunners of serving tables, side tables were made from the 16th century to stand against walls. Their backs are plain and there is often a drawer in the front frieze. The rectangular tops were made from planks.	Made from c.1700–50 for writing or dressing, lowboys usually have stretcher-less cabriole legs. The three top drawer fronts are often dummies applied to a single drawer.
WOOD	This varies according to date, but oak was commonly used.	Lowboys were made from oak, walnut or mahogany.
WHAT TO LOOK FOR	• Attractively shaped legs – these double baluster legs are a bonus. • Shaped stretcher (if there is one) – this X-frame stretcher adds charm and value. • Good patination – this adds greatly to value whatever the wood. • Original or appropriate handles – these pear-drops are replacements, but in keeping with the date of the table.	• Decorative details, such as ogee arches, or a frieze, as seen here. • Re-entrant corners (shaped corners on top). • Tops with moulded edges. • Outlines of overlapping drawer fronts on the carcass indicate authenticity.

objects, designed for the large rooms of grand Georgian houses; they were expensive items when made and have remained so.

It is hard to find small tables made in the 18th century for under £1000, and prime examples may fetch tens of thousands of pounds. If your budget is limited, however, you need not despair. The most successful 18th-century designs for small tables were often repeated in the late 19th century. These later versions are often extremely well made and offer you the opportunity to buy the elegance of 18th-century style at only a fraction of the cost. While a set of Georgian quartetto tables might cost £3,000 to £4,000, it should be possible for you to find an early 20th-century set for about £600 to £800.

Small tables are, in general, one of the most popular types of furniture. Their very portability means that they are taken from home to home rather than sold, which keeps both demand and prices high.

SILVER TABLES	CONSOLE TABLES	
  MAHOGANY SILVER TABLE c.1755 £15,000–25,000	 FRENCH c.1750 GILTWOOD CONSOLE TABLE £3,000–5,000	
Tables with galleried edges were designed by Chippendale in 1754; they were used for displaying objects and for serving tea in the 18th century. In the 19th century, French-style tables with metal galleries were popular.	With no back legs to support it, the console table was permanently fixed to a wall in an entrance hall or grand salon, often with a mirror above. Made from the 18th century onwards, they often came in pairs.	HOW, WHEN, WHY
Mahogany was used in the 18th century, and various woods after that.	Console tables are frequently found in giltwood or japanning, and often have marble tops.	WOOD
● Pierced galleries on 18th-century tables should be made from three thicknesses of laminated wood. ● Wide casters on 18th-century tables. ● Arresting decorative form – the delicate domed stretcher with urn finial is particularly attractive. ● Good-quality metal mounts on 19th-century versions.	● Original marble top in good condition. ● Pairs. ● Attractive carving, especially on the faces of figures – many (such as this one) are very ornate in the Italianate manner with swags, garlands, putti etc. Outspread eagle bases are also sought after.	WHAT TO LOOK FOR

OTHER SMALL TABLES II

PIER TABLES	TEA TABLES	COACH TABLES
ROSEWOOD PIER TABLE c.1820 £2,000–4,000	MAHOGANY TEA TABLE c.1820 £800–1,200	MAHOGANY COACH TABLE, c.1870 £400–600

HOW, WHEN, WHY

The pier is the wall space between two windows. Pier tables were made, usually in pairs, from the 18th century. They are similar to console tables, but have back supports.	Tables for serving tea date from the 18th century onwards (when tea-drinking became fashionable). Shapes vary – this one resembles a card table but, when opened, has a veneered top.	First popular in the mid- to late 19th century, coach tables are a variant of butlers' trays that could fold flat vertically when not in use. They were used for picnics in the garden or for eating in trains or mail coaches.

WOOD

Expensive woods were used, such as rosewood, mahogany and giltwood.	Mahogany was usually used for tea tables; japanning was popular in the 18th century.	Coach tables were commonly made from solid mahogany and had little decoration.

WHAT TO LOOK FOR

● Decorative appearance – semi-circular or serpentine shapes are desirable. ● Regency versions often have mirrors below to reflect light – original glass is a bonus. ● Original or traditional gilding. This one has been over-painted with gold and looks gaudy, detracting from its value.	● Well-figured wood. ● Swivel tops – these were added to some to make serving easier. ● Good decorative detail – the canted sabre legs on this one are an attractive feature. ● Original casters – these lion's paws are typical of the date.	● Examine the hinge on the folding flap to make sure that it is in good condition. ● Check that the top and base belong together – look underneath for any signs of tampering. ● Make sure that the legs and stretchers (if there are any) are sound.

OCCASIONAL TABLES	DISPLAY TABLES	QUARTETTO TABLES	
OCCASIONAL TABLE c.1880 £2,000–3,000	SATINWOOD DISPLAY TABLE c.1890 £1,000–1,500	MAHOGANY QUARTETTO TABLES, c.1910 £400–600	
The opulent French style of the 1720s and 1730s was enormously fashionable from 1830 to 1930; large numbers of small tables in the Louis XV manner such as this one (also known as *guéridons*) were made in England and France.	These are small tables with hinged glass tops that were used to display precious ornaments. Many were made in the last 15 years of Queen Victoria's reign and in the Edwardian era. French versions are called *vitrines*.	Nests of graduated tables were first made c.1780–1820 in England and revived in the last years of the 19th century. Practical for modern-day interiors, they have remained popular in the 20th century.	HOW, WHEN, WHY
Various woods were used and often combined to produce marquetry decoration.	Decorative woods – usually veneered and then sometimes painted – were used.	Mahogany was most common; papier mâché was used in the 19th century; satinwood is rare.	WOOD
● The top and platform stretchers should be of matching form; here, both are serpentine squares. ● Marquetry that is in good condition, with no pieces missing. ● Good-quality metal mounts. ● Sèvres-style porcelain plaques painted with attractive subjects.	● Elegant shape – the cabriole legs on this one are typical of the 1890s and reflect quality. ● Check that there are no chips or cracks in the glass – it could be expensive to replace. ● Attractive decoration – whether painted, gilt metal, marquetry or giltwood.	● Solid, generous proportions if they are Georgian – later versions tend to have thinner legs and lighter trestles. ● Reasonable condition – they are vulnerable to damage. ● Attractive painted decoration – in the French or neo-classical style.	WHAT TO LOOK FOR

Cabinets, Cupboards & Bookcases

A 'cabinet' was originally the name given to a small room, but, by the 17th century, small decorative cupboards with various drawers and compartments, known as cabinets, were symbols of wealth and prestige and among the most important pieces of furniture of the day. Cabinets were made only by the most highly skilled furniture makers. Hence the term 'cabinet-maker' came to mean a craftsman who was qualified to make the finest pieces of furniture.

Early bookcases reflect the fact that books were still the province of the wealthy, and the furniture made to hold them tended to be large and suitable for grand libraries and reading-rooms. As books became more affordable, the demand grew for bookcases of less opulent proportions, and a wide variety of smaller bookcases was made.

Bookcases with glazed tops from the 18th century are often used nowadays for displaying china, but there is also a plethora of display cabinets from the 19th century that were specifically designed for showing off a collection of china or other valuables. The delicacy and intricacy of the glazing bars add to the decorative appeal of cabinets and bookcases with glass doors. When purchasing, keep in mind that glazing bars with hexagonal, wavy or arched designs are more sought after and add more value than those of a simple, rectangular configuration.

CABINETS

Most cabinets have a strong architectural appearance, and their obvious decorative appeal has made them popular with both interior designers and antiques collectors.

All 17th- and 18th-century cabinets tend to be expensive. The famous Badminton cabinet was in fact the most expensive piece of furniture ever sold when it made over £8.5 million at Christie's auction house in London in 1990. However, purpose-built cabinets that were made in the late 19th and 20th centuries can still be found for modest sums and are worth acquiring.

▲ LACQUER CABINET
Lacquer cabinets were made in the Far East from the 17th century for export to the West, where they were mounted on European stands. This cabinet dates from c.1880, and both stand and cabinet were made in China. Red, blue, green and yellow lacquer is rarer than black, so this cabinet would fetch £3,000 to £4,000. Lacquered black, it would be worth only £1,000 to £1,500.

◀ CHINOISERIE
'Chinoiserie' is Oriental-style decoration made in Europe. This Chinese-style cabinet is faithfully based on an 18th-century design by Thomas Chippendale. On closer inspection, however, the bonded wood, machine-cut joints and brightly coloured gold paint point to the fact that it was made c.1985 for the decorative interior design market. If it had been made by Chippendale, it would be worth £30,000 or more; as it is, it would sell for between £1,500 and £2,000.

▼ MUSIC CABINET
Edwardian music cabinets (c.1900–1914) are rarely found in perfect condition; many have lost their top shelves and mirrors. The door is lined with pleated silk and conceals the velvet-lined shelves that stored sheet music.
£250–400

▲ TABLE CABINETS
17th-century Antwerp was the centre for the production of these small table cabinets, which were made from ebony and inlaid with engraved bone panels. Larger versions were also made and these were sometimes placed on stands, but even small pieces such as this one are rare and desirable today.
£3,000–5,000

▶ PROPORTIONS
This ebonized and painted cabinet was made c.1880. Its stylish decoration reflects the influence of the prominent Gothic Reform designer, Henry Stacey Marks RA. Over the years, however, it has been altered – the top has been re-ebonized and small circular marks suggest that there may once have been a shelf or some other superstructure behind it.
£150–250

COURT & PRESS CUPBOARDS

The term 'cup board' evolved from the earliest type of this furniture: a board or shelf used for storing cups or drinking vessels. Paradoxically, a 'court cup board' strictly speaking has no closed storage but just two or three open shelves. From the mid-17th century onwards, enclosed cupboards with slightly recessed tops were made. These are known as 'press cup boards', or erroneously termed court cupboards, and were among the most expensive and prestigious forms of furniture used for storage and display.

◀ **COURT CUPBOARDS**
This fine, early court cupboard, made c.1600, has the massive cup and cover supports that are typical of the period and sometimes also seen on trestle tables. On Victorian copies (or later pieces) the carving is often more complex.
£7,000–10,000

> **BEWARE**
> Look carefully at pre-1700 cupboards to make sure that there are genuine signs of age – imitations were produced in the late Victorian period, made up from early wood or wainscoting.

▼ **DECORATION**
Elements of architectural decoration, such as the broad pilasters and inverted breakfront corners, increase the value of this attractive early 18th-century press cupboard. Its warm golden colour is also a bonus.
£2,500–4,000

▲ **CONTINENTAL CUPBOARDS**
This elaborately carved cabinet was probably made in Malines, Belgium, where huge quantities of 17th-century-style carved oak furniture were made in the early 20th century.
£700–1,000

THE DATE (1667) ON
THIS SOLID OAK PRESS
CUPBOARD APPEARS TO
BE MORE OR LESS
ACCURATE — OFTEN
DATES ARE LATER
'IMPROVEMENTS'.

THE INITIALS 'RI'
AND 'TI' SUGGEST
THAT IT MAY HAVE
BEEN A WEDDING GIFT,
AND THE DATE MIGHT
BE THAT OF THE
COUPLE'S MARRIAGE.

This lunette carved
frieze is typical of the
Charles II period.

The hinges on these
doors are replacements.
Butterfly hinges, either
plain or with elaborately
curled tails, would have
been used at this date.

The columns are thinner
than those on the earlier
Elizabethan version (see
p.106, top left).

The simple 'joyned'
construction of the
doors is reminiscent
of panelling.

The warm, glowing
colour is just what you
should look for on early
oak furniture.

The stile legs have worn
away and metal casters
have been added to halt
the wear.

DECORATIVE MOTIFS

Strapwork

Lunette

Guilloche

WOODS
- Always solid and
not veneered.
- Nearly always oak.
- Elm occasionally used
for boards.

CORNER CUPBOARDS

Although they are undeniably attractive, corner cupboards can be a furniture dealer's nightmare. As rooms have become smaller, spare corners are harder to find and these cupboards have become more difficult to sell. Consequently, prices for them never seem to rise at the same rate as for other types of furniture. If you are lucky enough to have a corner to spare, you will find corner cupboards are very good value – even a pair of 18th-century corner cupboards can be fairly modestly priced. Most such cupboards on the market today date from the 18th and 19th centuries.

◀ STYLES
This unusual but pretty corner cupboard, made c.1770, looks like a corner washstand and may have been intended for a wash basin, jug or chamber pot. Apart from the top, all the lines are serpentine, and this stylistic feature makes the cupboard more valuable.
£1500–2,500

▲ HANGING CUPBOARDS
The simplest form of corner cupboard is the hanging variety with solid doors that was made from c.1700 until the mid-19th century; it was made in oak, mahogany and pine. If you look inside the cupboard and you are lucky, you might find that, as on this pine cupboard made c.1770, the original painted finish has survived.
£600–800

▶ CORNER BOOK CABINETS
This mahogany corner book cabinet, c.1910, was probably made in Germany, perhaps to fit around a column with three similar cabinets. The open shelves make this one of the most practical types of corner cupboard.
£2,500–3,500

STANDING CORNER CUPBOARDS WERE POPULAR IN THE GEORGIAN PERIOD. THIS MAHOGANY VERSION DATES FROM C.1785 AND IS WORTH ABOUT £2,000 TO £3,000.

The cornice hides the top, which would be left unfinished.

These attractive bars add to the value of the cupboard, as does the bow-front.

Shelves either follow the line of the outer carcass (here they are curved), or they are quite elaborately shaped.

Open the door and look obliquely at the glass. If you can see ripples and impurities, the glass is probably original – this is a bonus but not essential.

By the late 18th century, doors were hinged on the inside. On earlier 18th-century and provincial corner cupboards the hinges are on the outside of the doors.

BEWARE
Look out for marriages, where tops and bottoms do not belong together. Also, some hanging corner cupboards may simply be the top halves of standing corner cupboards.

DISPLAY CABINETS

A display cabinet is actually a vitrine; in other words, a cupboard with large glazed panels. Even though today they are often described as display cabinets, it seems likely that cabinets made in the 18th century were originally intended as bookcases. The fact that they were made for books is one reason why the shelves on even the most sophisticated Georgian cabinets do not necessarily line up with the glazing bars. Cabinets that were designed specifically for displaying objects only became common in the latter part of the 19th century.

▼ INLAYS

The satinwood and tulipwood crossbanding on this display cabinet is often thought to be a later feature, but it was extremely popular on provincial pieces that were made in Scotland and in the north of England c.1800.
£4,500–6,000

▲ DATING

The distinct contrast in graining and colour between the top and the base of this walnut-veneered cabinet points to the fact that they did not start life together. The top has simple, heavy glazing bars, typical of the early 18th century, and it probably came from a bureau or cabinet. The serpentine drawers, in contrast, would have been extremely rare at this date. The idealized Queen Anne-style stand was made during the 1920s.
£800–1,200

BEWARE

Many continental and 20th-century English display cabinets include panels of serpentine glass: make sure before you buy one that none of the glass panels is chipped – they can be very expensive to replace.

► MIRRORS

Mirror backs became popular features on display cabinets made from c.1850 onwards because they enabled you to see both sides of the objects that were being displayed; they also increased the light in the room. The thin legs, moulding and stringing, and the exaggerated swan-neck crest on this cabinet, which was produced c.1900, are weakened versions of late 18th-century styles. £700–1,000

▲ ART NOUVEAU CABINETS

Probably called 'Queen Anne' by its retailer, cabinets of this type were mass produced in the 1920s; they are becoming difficult to find in good original condition, however, and are probably sound investments for the future. The dramatic black roses are typical of the Art Nouveau style that waned just before World War I. £500–800

▼ ART DECO CABINETS

This walnut cabinet, made c.1930, is based on the radios of that period; it was designed by the Gordon Russell Workshops. A cabinet such as this would give an instant sense of the Art Deco period to any room. It would be good value at between £400 and £500.

CUPBOARDS & WARDROBES

The late 20th-century passion for fitted furniture has caused a fall in demand for antique wardrobes and cupboards. As a result, they often cost much less than their built-in modern equivalents – and you can take them with you when you move. Apart from being practical for storage, old wardrobes, especially those from continental Europe, are often extremely handsome pieces of furniture.

By the end of the 19th century, wardrobes tended to be made as parts of bedroom suites, not as individual pieces. The old 'clothes presses' were, by then, being used to store linen rather than clothing.

▼ WARDROBES

This classic mahogany wardrobe, made c.1780, would be a decorative and practical addition to any bedroom. Inside there are sliding trays above drawers, and a hanging space on each side. With wardrobes of this kind, the internal fittings have often been altered or removed, but, as long as this has been done in a sympathetic manner, the change should not greatly affect the value of the furniture.
£3,000–4,000

▲ FRENCH ARMOIRES

This oak and chestnut armoire, made c.1780, dates from the reign of Louis XVI. The long outset brass hinges and cockerel-head escutcheons are typical of the stylish metalware to be found on French furniture. The rococo carving also makes this a very attractive piece and it is worth around £3,000. A less elaborate version could be found for around £1,000.

BEWARE

● Some bookcases are wardrobes on which the solid doors have been replaced with glazed ones. This is acceptable if the piece is correctly described and priced fairly.
● When the popularity of the clothes press waned in the early 20th century, many had their tops cut off and discarded; the bottoms were converted into oddly proportioned chests of drawers.

▶ **CLOTHES PRESSES**
The word 'press' in this sense means a cupboard with shelves. Clothes presses with double doors, open shelves and low chests of drawers are usually made from mahogany and date from the Georgian period. This one is a provincial version made in Wales or Cheshire c.1780. In smaller country houses these cupboards were generally used to store the clothes of the whole family.
£2,000–3,000

◀ **DUTCH ARMOIRES**
Dutch armoires made in the 18th century, such as this one, made from oak c.1770, were always plain. If you find one with marquetry inlay, it is probably a modern reproduction, or it might have been 'improved' in the 19th century. Reproductions fetch about £2,500; a genuine piece from the 18th century, even with later inlay, might fetch £10,000.

WHAT IS THIS?
At first glance, this cupboard looks like the base of a 1770s press cupboard. However, if you look closely you will see that the proportions are wrong. In fact, it has been made up more recently from old bits of 18th-century wood to act as a video or TV cabinet. While it might be practical, it is not a piece that will increase in value.
£300–400

BOOKCASES

Before choosing a bookcase, make sure that it is not a wardrobe that has had its upper doors glazed, as this was a fairly common alteration in the 19th century.

The top glazed section of an 18th-century bookcase is usually narrower than the base. Early bookcases tend to have small panes of glass (see below). On both later Victorian and modern versions, the glass is more likely to be made from a single sheet; the glazing bars then sit on the surface of this glass.

Gothic Revival bookcases dating from the 1840s with glazed doors and fitted with adjustable shelves are particularly desirable.

► PINE BOOKCASES

This is the *crème de la crème* of pine bookcases made c.1780 and based on a design by Thomas Chippendale. Although now stripped, originally it would have been painted to fit in with the decor of the room. Even so, it is still in good condition and would be worth £7,000 to £10,000. A similar version that was 'made-up' from old wood would cost £2,000 to £3,000.

CONSTRUCTION

Individual panes of glass are puttied into the glazing bars on early bookcases.

◄ DOUBLE-SIDED BOOKCASES

This late 18th-century mahogany double-sided open bookcase needs a large room – it measures 3 ft 7 in (110 cm) high and 3 ft 3 in (101 cm) wide. It is lucky to have escaped a dealer's saw: sliced down the middle it would make two bookcases. Attractive pieces of furniture that hold books are highly sought after, so this is a valuable piece.
£4,000–5,000

DATING
On bookcases with open doors, the joint on the corners of the door frame helps with dating. This example has a 90° joint, popular during the late 18th century.

▶ REVOLVING BOOKCASES
The innovative revolving bookcase became popular in the 1820s and was refined by the Victorians and Edwardians. This early example was made around 1820 and has three independently revolving tiers and dummy book supports; because of its quality it is worth £7,000 to £10,000. A Victorian version would cost between £3,000 and £5,000 and an Edwardian example £2,000 to £4,000.

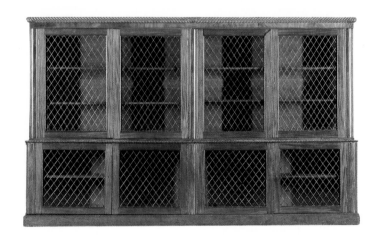

▲ OPEN BOOKCASES
The design of this German mahogany-veneered open bookcase, made c.1820, reflects the Empire taste with its severe shape and heavy gilt mounts. Although stylish, this is a fairly inexpensive piece – the pine carcass is unfinished inside. £1,500–2,500.

▲ ALTERATIONS
The proportions of this Victorian mahogany bookcase, made c.1850, look wrong, and closer inspection shows that the upper doors have been carefully reduced in height – probably to fit in a room with a low ceiling. Later alterations such as this can reduce the value of a piece considerably. £3,000–5,000

Dressers were made from the 17th century onwards and could be found in the dining-rooms and kitchens of more modest homes throughout the 19th century. As with most country furniture, styles tended to change little over time but were influenced by the region where the dresser was made; it is often easier to tell the place of origin of a dresser rather than the date of manufacture. High dressers (with racks) and low dressers (without racks) are among the most popular pieces of furniture today. Surprisingly versatile wherever you put them, this probably explains why they have always been comparatively expensive items.

During the 18th century, as imported mahogany became available, mahogany serving tables and sideboards became fashionable pieces for stylish dining-rooms. Serving tables are long, narrow tables that were designed, as the name suggests, for serving and preparing food. Although not as practical as sideboards, they can be among the most attractive of tables. Some have elaborately carved legs and friezes that are embellished with a variety of garlands and masks.

An enormous range of side cabinets was made during the Victorian period, many of them lavishly decorated with marquetry, porcelain plaques and metal mounts.

HIGH DRESSERS

Many high dressers started life without racks; these were added later, taken from other dressers or made up of old wood. If the alteration is sympathetic and was done some time ago, it can be difficult to detect and does not affect the value much.

Nearly all early dressers were made from oak. Elm was occasionally used for boards, and if you find one with parts made from yew, it will raise the price considerably. Still a popular form, many pine and painted pine dressers are being made today in response to demand from the lower end of the market.

▲ **LEGS**
Some of the most expensive dressers are those with cabriole legs. Dressers of this type usually date from the mid-18th century. This one has the added novelty of cupboard doors on either side of the rack. Its value is reduced because there is a piece missing from the cornice, possibly because it has been fitted into an alcove. Note, too, how the proportions of the piece are rather squat. £3,000–5,000

IN SOUTHERN ENGLAND, RACKS ON DRESSERS WERE USUALLY OPEN, BUT THE BOARDED BACK WAS POPULAR ON WELSH DRESSERS, SUCH AS THIS 19TH-CENTURY EXAMPLE (RIGHT). AS SKIRTING BOARDS BECAME POPULAR, DRESSERS WERE PULLED AWAY FROM THE WALL AND OPEN BACKS WERE FILLED IN WITH BOARDS.

◄ **STYLE**
The architectural proportions of this 18th-century painted pine dresser raise it from a simple country piece to an elegant designer item. For many collectors the original painted finish also adds greatly to the appeal of the piece; if repainted, this dresser would lose value. As it is, the piece is worth £4,000 to £5,000; it would cost £1,500 to £2,500 if repainted.

WHAT TO LOOK FOR
• Matching decorative motifs on the top and base, which show that the two parts belong together.
• Signs that the piece has been used: knife marks, scratches from pots etc.
• Plenty of encrusted dirt in the grooves and corners.

► **WELSH DRESSERS**
Prices vary according to the decorative appeal of a piece. This one has attractive arched panelling on the doors, increasing its value.
£3,000–3,500

OTHER WELSH PIECES
The tridarn, with its three tiers of shelves and cupboards, and the deuddarn, a type of court cupboard, were among other pieces of country dining-room or kitchen furniture made in Wales.

LOW DRESSERS

Low dressers are as sought after as their high counterparts, and there seems to be little difference between the prices achieved for the two types. Low dressers, however, are arguably more versatile and sophisticated.

Most low dressers cost between £1,000 and £5,000. Low dressers from the 17th century are the rarest examples, although not necessarily the most expensive. Prices are boosted by decorative details such as friezes, carved or inlaid decoration and, above all, a good, mellow colour.

Provincial houses in the late 18th century favoured the dresser, rather than the sideboard, for the dining-room. You were more likely to find a basic, working dresser in the kitchen.

▲ EARLY LOW DRESSERS
Low dressers from the William and Mary period (late 17th century), such as this one, are rare and can be dated from the legs. The baluster legs seen here predate the cabriole legs seen on the example shown right. The heavily-mitred drawers are similar to those seen on 17th-century chests of drawers. £3,000–4,000

▼ ALTERATIONS
This solid oak low dresser, made c.1800, would originally have had a rack (which has been sawn off). You can see the moulding and the remnants of a plate holder, and, arguably, it might be better to have it completely removed. Obviously, the price is reduced by this defect, but, perhaps surprisingly, not dramatically so. £2,500–3,000

The large brass handles and escutcheons are of the period and appear to be original.

THIS OAK DRESSER DATES FROM
c.1770 AND HAS MANY DECORATIVE
FEATURES THAT MAKE IT
PARTICULARLY DESIRABLE.
£3,000–4,000

PROPORTIONS

Note that most dressers (high or low) have three drawers across their width. A dresser that has only two drawers should be carefully examined to see if it has been reduced in width.

Although the cornice is plain in design, the frieze below has been crossbanded in mahogany.

The solid oak drawer fronts are decorated with fruitwood banding and fan medallions in each spandrel.

The wavy line of the apron softens the overall appearance and adds style.

The front legs are elegantly curved in the cabriole style. With the introduction of cabriole legs, the central legs and stretchers seen on earlier examples (such as the one opposite) were no longer used.

Although there are appropriate signs of wear, the pad feet are still in good condition.

WHAT'S INSIDE?

The inside of the drawers should look dry, with no signs of staining or tampering. Pull out the drawer and check that the wood is all of a similar colour, and that the dovetails were coarsely hand-cut.

EARLY SIDEBOARDS

Sophisticated and elegant, 18th-century serving tables and sideboards are classic pieces of dining-room furniture and prices tend to reflect their popularity. Most cost between £3,000 and £10,000; small pieces are particularly sought after since they are better-suited to modern houses.

The earliest examples date from c.1750, when long, narrow tables flanked by urns on pedestal cupboards became fashionable. Sideboards were designed to suit the needs of 18th-century upper-class society: to hold the silver, china, tablecloths, bottles and other accoutrements necessary for dining.

Most English sideboards have brass galleries that originally would have been hung with silk curtains to protect the wallpaper from the juices that splashed as the meat was being carved. Dining was a lengthy process in wealthy homes during the 18th century, and sideboards usually had cellaret drawers on one side for storing wine and cupboards on the other side for storing chamber pots.

The shape of a sideboard, as well as the figure of the wood, can have a dramatic affect on the value of a piece: serpentine and bow-fronted versions are more expensive than pieces with straight fronts.

◀ **BOW-FRONTED SIDEBOARDS**
This is an 18th-century bow-fronted, mahogany sideboard (c.1770). Although it looks as if there are two drawers on each side, these are actually dummy fronts and there is only one deep drawer. On later versions the central arch became a little lower and was often turned into a drawer without a handle.
£3,000–5,000

BEWARE
Turned legs, a feature of later sideboards, were often replaced with the earlier square tapering style of leg to make 19th-century sideboards look older (and more valuable). The legs should form part of the carcass and not be joined onto it. On this altered example you can also see a marked difference in the colour of the wood.
£700–1,000

◀ LATER INLAYS

This serpentine sideboard, like the bow-fronted one opposite, was made c.1770. However, this example has a more desirable shape. During the 19th century it was 'improved' with satinwood inlay. Although a purist might think that this alteration reduces the value, it appeals to some decorators and therefore will not affect the price unduly.
£3,000–4,000

DO NOT WORRY IF...

the somewhat awkward deep drawers have been converted into cupboards. This is a common alteration and does not seriously affect value.

▶ LEGS

This mahogany sideboard, made c.1810, retains its original brass gallery; it also has its original turned legs with reeding that continues to the top. It is a quality piece, and the fact that it is unaltered raises its value.
£6,000–8,000.

◀ SERVING TABLES

Until the 1960s, serving tables, such as this mahogany example, made c.1830 by Gillow of Lancaster, were considered second best to sideboards and were much less valuable. Recently, however, they have regained popularity, and there is no longer a great difference in price.
£3,000–4,000

LATER SIDEBOARDS

A wide variety of sideboards was produced during the 19th century, including the heavy pedestal versions that were made during the reign of William IV, and the eclectic range of styles such as Gothic Reform, Art Nouveau, neo-rococo and Sheraton Revival that were made during Queen Victoria's reign and into the Edwardian period.

Many of the sideboards made in the 19th century were well over 84 in (215 cm) long; they can be overpowering if they are placed in modern dining-rooms. Nevertheless, if you can find one to fit, they tend to cost about half as much as those made in the 18th century and are extremely practical for both storage and display purposes.

◄ EARLY VICTORIAN PEDESTAL SIDEBOARDS
The charm of this piece is its small size: it is only 48 in (122 cm) wide. Sideboards such as this one were popular throughout the first half of the 19th century, so they can be difficult to date accurately. The heavy pedestals on this one, however, point to a date of c.1840 (an earlier version would be lighter).
£700–1,000

▲ PEDESTAL SIDEBOARDS
Until very recently, early 19th-century mahogany pedestal sideboards, such as this one, have been very difficult to sell; this is in spite of the fact that they are invariably of fine quality and in their day were high fashion pieces. Note, however, that Victorian sideboards are not always of this quality.
£5,000–10,000

◀ **ARTS AND CRAFTS SIDEBOARDS**
This chunky, solid-oak Arts and Crafts sideboard, made c.1870, with its panelled doors and medieval-inspired decoration, may have been designed by the architect Charles Bevan, who was one of the pioneers of this style of furniture, known as Gothic Reform.
£1,500–2,000

THE ARTS AND CRAFTS MOVEMENT

In reaction to the industrialization of the 19th century, designers such as William Morris (1834–1896) placed greater emphasis on hand craftsmanship and furniture of simple design that was unspoiled by staining or similar preparations. This led to a revival in traditional methods of construction that was to prove popular throughout Europe. The Arts Workers' Guild was founded in 1884; four years later the Arts and Crafts Exhibition Society held its first show.

▲ **STYLES**
Some late Victorian sideboards reflect the styles of the previous century; the shape of the base of this one, made c.1890, with its tapering legs and spade feet, is very similar to those made in the 1770s. However, the high back, bevelled oval mirror and elaborate inlays found on this sideboard are very much in the tradition and style of the late Victorian and Edwardian eras.
£1,500–2,500

SIDE CABINETS

Although side cabinets were first produced in the 18th century, they were not particularly fashionable until the early 19th century, when the range available grew dramatically.

The late Victorians and Edwardians were especially fond of side cabinets made with mirror backs and used them for displaying decorative objects. By the late 19th century, many of the side cabinets being made were elaborately decorated. It is important to check a piece's condition carefully before buying, as damage to the inlay, carving or mounts will require expensive restoration work.

The word 'credenza' was popularized by the Victorians. Borrowed from the Italian, it originally referred to 16th-century sideboards.

◀ GEORGIAN SIDE CABINETS
Side cabinets of the 18th century are not common and tend to be far simpler than those made in the following century. This one, made c.1770, has cupboard doors enclosing shelves and drawers (including a bottle drawer). The proportions look slightly odd because the feet have been reduced by 3–4in (8–10cm), lowering the piece's value.
£1,500–2,500

▶ ROSEWOOD
Rosewood, a figured dark red-brown wood used for this c.1830 chiffonier, was imported in large quantities from South America in the early 19th century. It is found in good-quality furniture made between 1800 and 1840.
£2,000–3,000

CHIFFONIERS
Chiffoniers originated in France, where the word denotes a small cabinet for storing everyday bric-a-brac. Two types were made in England: those with cupboard doors below and stepped shelves above; and those with flat tops that often had book shelves on each side of the central doors.

◀ BOULLE

Boulle marquetry is made by cutting a pattern from thin sheets of brass overlaid on red or coloured tortoiseshell. This technique was perfected in France by André-Charles Boulle in the late 17th century; it became popular in England in the early 18th century, when this cabinet was made.
£2,000–3,000

BEWARE

● Before buying boulle, check that the brass is not lifting – it can be very expensive to repair.
● Make sure that no glass is broken.
● If you intend taking tortoiseshell out of the EC, you will need to obtain a special licence.

▲ FRENCH-STYLE

This walnut-veneered side cabinet, or credenza, made c.1850, has attractive tulipwood crossbanding and gilt-metal mounts. These decorations reflect the Victorians' love of French style. The plaques are copies of Sèvres porcelain.
£2,500–4,000

◀ LATER CABINETS

Towards the end of the 19th century, many side cabinets gained upper sections of shelves, mirrors and porcelain niches. Made from rosewood, this one is lavishly inlaid with classical revival marquetry.
£1,000–2,000

CREDENZAS

Many Victorian credenzas were built with large mirrors above. You can usually see signs of where they were originally fitted to the tops of the cabinets.

The precursor of the bureau was the writing slope: a portable and slant-lidded box that was hinged at the top. During the 17th century, as householders became more settled, writing slopes on stands or chests of drawers began to appear.

Writing furniture evolved hand in hand with cupboards and cabinets during the 17th century. By the reign of Queen Anne, walnut-veneered bureaux had become popular.

Throughout the 18th century, writing furniture became more varied and sophisticated. Bureaux were combined with shelves for books to make bureau bookcases, and pedestal desks appeared.

A new form of writing furniture that appeared in the 18th century was the Carlton House desk. This grand, D-shaped writing table, surmounted by a curved bank of drawers and compartments, was so called because the first one was believed to have been designed for the Prince Regent. Other Regency innovations in writing furniture include the *bonheur du jour*, an elegant ladies' desk, and the davenport (see p.130).

All writing furniture is keenly sought after today and prices can be high for quality pieces. If you want a desk to fit in an alcove, always remember to measure it across the feet, because generally the feet stick out further than the rest of the desk. Also, be sure to measure the alcove from inside the skirting boards.

BUREAUX

The bureau is certainly the most common and practical type of writing furniture. The top is a steeper version of the 17th-century writing box while the base is a chest of drawers. Early bureaux were often made in two parts, with the join concealed by moulding. The upper part, fitted with pigeon holes and drawers, often had a secret compartment. Size, as always, affects value: a bureau under 3 ft (92 cm) wide is particularly desirable because it will fit more easily into today's smaller rooms.

▲ OAK BUREAUX
The wood on the lid of this attractive mid-18th-century oak bureau has been cut so that its medullary rays (graining) are revealed.

The shaped bracket feet are surprisingly high; the fact that they have survived without being cut down is no less remarkable.
£1,000–1,500

◀ MAHOGANY BUREAUX
When you open a bureau, always pull out one or, preferably, both lopers (supports) and examine the hinges to make certain that they are in good condition. This is a classic mahogany bureau that was made about 1780.
£1,200–1,800

▼ DUTCH BUREAUX
This bureau, produced c.1710, would have been plain with no inlay or stringing; the decoration is a 19th-century addition. It was probably made in the Netherlands, but it is hard to be certain of this because many Dutch craftsmen came to England, bringing their cabinet-making techniques with them. Most Dutch bureaux are very large by comparison with their English counterparts. £3,000–5,000

▲ BUREAUX DE DAME
Bureaux de dame (ladies' desks) were popular in continental Europe in the late 19th and early 20th centuries; often extremely decorative, they are good value in today's market. This French version, made c.1890, is *bombé* in form and elaborately inlaid, pushing its price up to £2,500 to £3,000. You can find some simpler versions that will cost around £1,500.

SIGNS OF QUALITY
- Stylish interiors: perhaps with arched or stepped compartments or decorated with marquetry – hidden drawers are a bonus.
- Concealed writing well.
- Attractively-figured veneers.

BUREAU BOOKCASES

The most important thing to check before buying a bureau bookcase is that it is not a 'marriage'. Look at the sides to make sure that the grain and colour of the wood are similar at the top and bottom, and that there are no signs of tampering. Looking at the back of the piece can be misleading – the two parts do not always match. The upper part may be panelled, as it is visible through the glazing; the back of the base is usually made from unfinished flat boards.

By the 19th century a piece of this form was known as a 'secretary'. A wider version was known as a 'gentleman's secretary'.

▶ **MARRIAGES**
The base of this bureau bookcase is mostly 18th century but the rather odd proportions of the upper part show that it dates from the 20th century. This piece probably started life as a bureau, without any bookcase, and at the same time that the top was added the lower half was embellished with marquetry.
£1,000–1,500

▼ **VALUE**
This must be one of the least expensive bureau bookcases around. Made c.1920 from oak, and stained to make it look old, it has panelled drawers that imitate the Jacobean style, while the leaded panes are reminiscent of the type of glass that you would see in front doors of the same date.
£200–300

◀ **LATER STYLES**
This bureau bookcase, made c.1940 by Heal's of Tottenham Court Road, London, is a modern design based on the traditional 18th-century form. The solid oak has been limed to give a light, dry look to the wood. The use of a plinth rather than feet adds weight to the overall effect.
£700–1,000

THIS IS A CLASSIC
18TH-CENTURY
BUREAU BOOKCASE,
MADE C.1780.
THE BEST GEORGIAN
EXAMPLES ARE OFTEN
LARGER THAN THOSE
OF THE EARLIER AND
LATER PERIODS.
THIS ONE IS A FAIRLY
AVERAGE SIZE AND
MEASURES 7 FT 8 IN
(234 CM) HIGH BY 3 FT
3 IN (99 CM) WIDE.
£3,000–5,000

The detachable pierced
swan neck crest is a
decorative feature that
adds value.

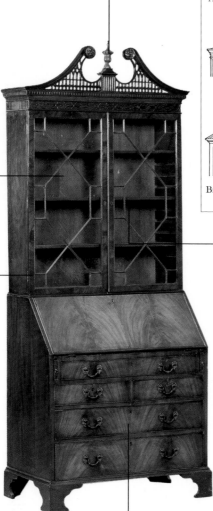

CRESTINGS CAN HELP WITH DATING

American bonnet
1730–1760

Double Dome
1690–1720

Swan neck
pediment
1760–1810

Moulded detail
1780–1810

Broken pediment
1730–1800

Regency
1800–1830

As with many bureau
bookcases, this one has
13 panels of glass in
each door.

The top part is
typically slightly
narrower than the
base, and there is a lip
moulding concealing
the join.

The shelves are
usually adjustable and
supported by pegs.
Examine the shelves
carefully – if the piece
has been cut down,
the shelves will have
been trimmed too.

BEWARE
If the sides of the
top and bottom
are flush, this
might imply a
marriage, or that
the piece has
been reduced
in size.

The patination and
colour of the veneers
are important on such
an imposing piece of
furniture. Here, they are
particularly well chosen;
note the way in which
the lid and drawer
fronts complement one
another.

DAVENPORTS

The davenport, one of the most popular small pieces of writing furniture, was named after Captain Davenport, for whom the first one was made, by Gillow of Lancaster, in the late 18th century. The best davenports can fetch £3,000 or more; a lesser version could cost as little as £500. Most are very elaborate, typifying the High Victorian style.

▶ PIANO TOPS
Piano top davenports are so called because of the curved shape of the top of the writing surface. They are also sometimes known as 'harlequin' davenports;

they were given this name because they have stationery compartments that push down into the main carcass and pop up at the release of a button.
£2,500–3,000

◀ REGENCY DAVENPORTS
This early Regency davenport, made c.1820, is much plainer in style than most later versions; it has a writing surface on runners that pulls

out over your knees. This example is made of mahogany, but davenports were also made of rosewood, satinwood and walnut. It would cost between £1,800 and £2,500.

▶ VALUE
Even though this 19th-century davenport is in a rather sorry state, with one or two handles missing, the serpentine top and cabriole legs add to

its value. This piece would fetch around £1,000 to £1,500 at an auction even in this condition; if the legs were straight, it would fetch less – between £800 and £1,200.

ROLL TOPS

Roll tops are derived from the grandest of desks that were used by kings to stand beside when they received guests. The most famous one of all is the *Bureau du Roi* at Versailles. Apart from such exceptional pieces with important provenance, prices for roll tops are generally lower than those paid for slant-lid bureaux because there is a tendency for the cylinders in roll tops to jam.

▼ FRENCH ROLL TOPS

This beautifully made French desk, from c.1900, copies a style that was first seen in the 1780s. The figure of the mahogany is particularly attractive; it is known as 'plum pudding' mahogany. £3,000–5,000

▼ SHERATON REVIVAL

This Edwardian Sheraton-style roll top desk is made from an East Indian satinwood that is a much deeper colour than you would find on an original 18th-century piece. The small proportions also tell you that it is from a later period. If the desk had been made in the 18th century it would be far larger and grander. £1,500–2,000

▶ VALUE

This oak roll top desk, produced c.1910, was probably made as a functional piece of office furniture. It is in excellent condition and would be good value at £150 to £200. If it had two pedestals, it would be worth somewhat more.

PEDESTAL DESKS

The English pedestal desk, still a popular type of office furniture, was introduced in the 1670s. Georgian and Regency pedestal desks with leather-lined tops and well-figured veneers offer elegance and utility. Some were designed to be free standing and have drawers on one side and cabinets on the other; some are known as partners' desks and can be used by two people at the same time. Partners' desks usually have drawers on both sides of the frieze, and their pedestals have drawers on one side and cupboards on the other. The cupboards sometimes have dummy drawer fronts.

◀ KNEE-HOLE DESKS
Small desks such as this one, made from mahogany c.1800, are sometimes called knee-hole desks. This one is a partners' desk because the opposite side has cupboards and drawers.
£3,000–4,000

▼ SERPENTINE DESKS
This is a late Victorian copy of the grandest form of 1740s Georgian partners' desk. The serpentine-shaped top raises the value to between £20,000 and £25,000. If it was a Georgian piece, it could make £100,000 or more.

CONSTRUCTION
The back of a pedestal desk was either plainly veneered, so that it could stand by a window, or, if it was to stand against a wall, left unfinished.

◀ GILLOW DESKS

The Victorians 'improved' the simple Georgian pedestal design by adding a gallery and banks of drawers on top, and an upholstered footrest in the space between the pedestals. This fine-quality desk was made by Gillow of Lancaster c.1870. Typically, the central drawer is stamped with the firm's name. £2,500–4,000

▼ KIDNEY-SHAPED DESKS

The kidney form was and still is a popular shape usually seen on small drawing-room pieces. This late Victorian example, constructed c.1900, is made of mahogany decorated with engraved boxwood inlay. £4,000–5,000

QUALITY FEATURES
- Metal mounts or carved decoration.
- Good-quality locks – perhaps marked by the locksmith.
- Desirable shapes: serpentine or kidney.

OTHER WRITING FURNITURE

Among the more varied types of writing furniture are *secretaires*. These desks usually take the form of flat-fronted cabinets with deep drawer fronts; the drawer fronts conceal stationery compartments and pull out to form smooth writing surfaces.

However, *secretaire* drawers were often added to smaller pieces of furniture such as chiffoniers or chests of drawers, and this adds to their value. Nonetheless, bureaux are generally more sought after than *secretaires*.

Writing tables, inspired by the French *bureau plat,* were also popular in England from c.1740. Similar to library tables, they have drawers fitted for stationery and leather tops that, in the 18th century, would often have been covered in baize.

Towards the end of the 18th century, and once again a hundred years later, D-shaped writing tables with curving bands of drawers were popular; these were known as Carlton House desks (see also p.126).

▶ **SECRETAIRE BOOKCASES**
The *secretaire* bookcase first became popular during the late 18th century. This one was made c.1800 from mahogany and has cupboard doors below enclosed shelves; some have drawers instead.
£2,500–3,500

◀ **SECRETAIRES**
The awkward design of *secretaires* such as this one has the disadvantage of making the desk unstable when the flap is used as a writing surface. Prices tend to be lower than for bureaux, although the figuring of the wood and the quality of the metal mounts add to the desirability and value of this one.
£1,200–1,800

▶ BONHEUR DU JOUR

This little *bonheur du jour* looks as though it should be French but it was actually made in England c.1840, at the height of the Victorians' passion for French taste. Writing cabinets of this type were made for ladies' drawing-rooms; this one has a leather-lined pull-out writing slide.
£3,000–4,000

◀ CARLTON HOUSE DESKS

This version of the Carlton House desk, based on Sheraton and Hepplewhite designs, dates from c.1900. It was made by Gillow of Lancaster.
£4,000–6,000

▶ WRITING TABLES

This mahogany writing table is a copy of one of the earliest forms, dating from c.1740. Dealers often call later copies 'Victorian', but, like many others, this one was made between 1910 and 1920.
£1,500–2,000

More elaborate early beds have solid headboards and two pillars supporting deep carved friezes and ceilings called 'testers', hence the term 'tester bed'. Opulent draperies, an essential part of the design of beds, could be drawn to enclose the occupants, protecting them from draughty bed-chambers.

A popular variation from the late 17th century, the half-tester bed, has no foot posts, although the tester still covers most of the bed. On later versions, the tester often covers only half of the bed.

Until the introduction of sprung mattresses in the 19th century, mattresses were usually stuffed with straw and supported on wooden lathes or ropes. Beds would have been much more comfortable after the introduction of springs. Today, antique beds are usually fitted with modern sprung mattresses that sit on top of the original bed rails (supports).

Before you buy an antique bed, measure it to make sure that it is big enough. Many 'double' beds measure about 4ft wide (121cm) by 6ft (182cm) long and are rather small by modern standards.

Among other types of bedroom furniture you might come across are wardrobes, dressing tables, washstands, commodes and bed-steps. Less expensive bedroom furniture was often made of pine and originally was painted.

EARLY BEDS

It is surprising that, compared with other types of antique furniture, beds are quite rare. Early examples are almost impossible to find unaltered and, as a result, there is a plethora of 'made-up' beds put together with wood taken from other pieces of furniture.

Early beds have very heavy bedposts that are often elaborately turned and carved. As the centuries progressed, posts became more slender and elegant (see box below).

Half-headed bedsteads, with no testers and low headboards, could be found in the homes of the less wealthy from Elizabethan times. The rails of the bedstead were pierced to take rope supports that held rudimentary stuffed or woven mattresses.

▲ **ALTERATIONS**
The headboard on this tester bed is made in the same way as wainscoting. In common with many 17th-century oak beds, this one has been reassembled from parts of an old bed and panelling.
£3,000–4,000

◀ **GEORGIAN BEDS**
Overall, this is a good-quality late Georgian bed with attractive spirally reeded pillars. However, the giltwood cornice is a later Victorian addition, and reduces the bed's value, although the original 19th-century hangings are a definite bonus.
£2,500–3,500

MATTRESSES
Old beds are not generally made to standard modern sizes. If buying one, take into account the cost of having a mattress specially made. You also need to add the cost of a quilt or coverlet and hangings if you are buying a high post bed with a tester.

▶ **RESTORATION**
This four-poster bed, made from mahogany c.1835, has been extensively restored. The upholstery would not be to everyone's taste, but the size of the bed (it measures 6 ft 2 in (2 m) long), and the fact that it is sold with its mattress, makes it good value at between £3,000 and £5,000.

BED POSTS
The style of the bed posts can give a clue to the date of the bed:

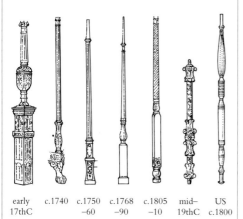

early 17thC	c.1740	c.1750 –60	c.1768 –90	c.1805 –10	mid– 19thC	US c.1800

LATER BEDS

Bed design changed dramatically in the 19th century as a result of improvements made in manufacturing. Tubular brass beds were made from around 1820 onwards. As metal casting techniques improved later in the century, cast iron beds became quite popular.

Less expensive beds were also made from steel tubing plated in brass. The prices of all these metal beds tend to be lower than those of wooden beds, even though many of them have survived unaltered. Take care if you buy one, as they have also been reproduced.

Wooden beds, of course, were still made. Mahogany was commonly used but pine and even papier mâché were also popular, as were beds with padded, upholstered headboards.

◀ **BRASS BEDS**
The fine quality of this stylish brass single bed, one of a pair produced c.1890, is reflected in the unusual Maltese cross decoration and the sturdy brass columns. It was sold by Maple & Co. (top furniture retailers) and the labels are still present.
£1,500–2,000 (for the pair)

▼ **CAMPAIGN BEDS**
Campaign beds were designed to be taken apart quickly for easy transportation – to the battlefield if necessary. This 19th-century black-painted iron and brass example has survived complete with a vintage Heal's mattress.
£800–1,200.

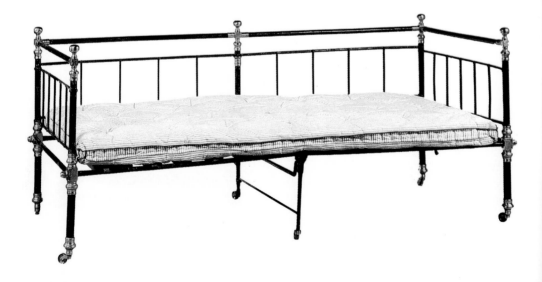

◀ FRENCH BEDS
Made from richly coloured
mahogany, this French Empire
bed, produced c.1810, has been
applied with fine-quality *bronze
doré* (ormolu) mounts. Beds of
this type can be used as settees,
but, because they are the size of
very small double beds, prices
tend to be relatively low.
£3,000–4,000

◀ SIZE
Although highly decorative, this
French kingwood veneered bed,
made c.1910 in the 18th-century
style, is only 4ft 5in (135cm)
wide. This is an awkward size
for modern-day use; the price
would more than double if it
were 'king-sized'.
£4,000–6,000

▶ AMERICAN BEDS
Surprisingly, American furniture
is relatively inexpensive on the
British market. This double bed,
made during the 19th century,
reflects the influence of the
designer Bruce Talbert. Beds in
the Aesthetic taste increase in
value when signed or firmly
attributed to a specific maker.
£2,000–3,000

BEDROOM SUITES

A bedroom suite usually comprises either a double bed or a pair of single beds, a wardrobe, a dressing table and a pair of bedside tables. Suites made before plumbing was a standard fixture in middle-class homes (in other words, the mid-19th century) might have washstands as well. Most suites date from the early Victorian period onwards,

and prices can be surprisingly reasonable today. For instance, you can often buy a whole suite for the same price that you would pay for two or three pieces separately. The most popular items in a suite are pairs of small bedside cabinets; chests of drawers and dressing tables come next. Single beds are almost impossible to sell on their own.

▲ **PROVENANCE**
These items are part of a six-piece suite in pine, painted with original Grecian-style decoration, made by Thomas Schoolbred, c.1880. A suite such as this would usually cost £1,500 to £2,000. However, when this one was included in a well-publicized house-sale (at Stokesay Court, Shropshire) its price more than doubled to £4,025.

▲ **PAINTED SUITES**
Bedroom suites that have survived with their original painted decoration intact are worth looking out for.

This suite, painted with an original Chinoiserie design, dates from c.1900 and consists of seven pieces.
£1,000–1,500

▶ **VALUE**
The value of this late 19th-century dressing table is dramatically boosted by the fact that it was made by the leading furniture makers, Howard & Sons, from top-quality Oregon pine, and has survived with its original finish intact. Stripped, this piece would be worth about 75 per cent less. It is also part of a suite that consists of a dressing table, two bedside cupboards and a towel rail. The dressing table alone would sell for £2,000 to £2,500.

◀ **CABINETS**
Bedside cabinets are usually the most valuable part of a suite and this French kingwood-veneered example, made c.1855, would be worth more if there were a second one. It is part of a suite that is worth £3,000 to £4,000.

▶ **ART DECO SUITES**
This Art Deco dressing table is part of a suite made in the 1930s. Although commercially made, with machine-cut birch veneered onto plywood, this suite is very stylish; you might pay £2,000 to £2,500 for the suite with matching wardrobe, bed, cabinets and dressing table.

DRESSING TABLES

Dressing tables of the 18th century or earlier are relatively rare and tend to prove expensive because of their age and quality.

Early dressing tables were made to be covered with rich tablecloths on which toilet accessories could be arranged. Many of them are multi-purpose and include writing slides and deep drawers that held wash basins. Dressing tables of both the Victorian and Edwardian eras were made in large numbers, and, unless particularly stylish, can be picked up very reasonably.

▶ MAHOGANY DRESSING TABLES

Made c.1820, this solid mahogany table appears to be multi-purpose: in terms of form, it is similar to contemporary sideboards and it could serve as a small side table. However, the gallery along the top of the table suggests that it was used primarily as a dressing table. Many such tables have been altered: they tend to become leather-lined desks, which are more saleable.
£1,500–2,000

◀ PAINTED DRESSING TABLES

This painted dressing table, made c.1870 (almost certainly as part of a suite), was probably intended for a secondary or servant's bedroom. It still has its original mirror, and the painted finish with its attractive 'malachite' border adds value; however, the paint has suffered some water damage (see p.34).
£600–900

BEWARE

Dressing tables sometimes have their superstructures removed and their tops lined in leather to make them into desks. Plugged holes are evidence of this.

◀ FRENCH DRESSING TABLES
The presence of a writing slide will add considerable value to even the most ordinary dressing table. This attractive rosewood-veneered example, made c.1880, has inexpensive metal machine-made mounts but would still be worth £2,500 to £3,500. If the writing slide was missing, it would cost around £1,000 less.

◀ VALUE
This dressing table, produced c.1900, is stamped with a Liberty's label that adds to its value. Prices for much early 20th-century furniture can be surprisingly modest and well-designed pieces such as this dressing table are probably good investments for the future.
£500–700

▲ ART NOUVEAU DRESSING TABLES
This stylish oak dressing table is a typical Art Nouveau piece. It was made c.1910 by Heal's, a leading furniture retailer of the period based in London's Tottenham Court Road.
£200–300

LIBERTY & CO.
Founded by Arthur Lasenby Liberty in 1875, this well-known company, based in London's Regent Street, commissioned Arts and Crafts-style furniture, as well as fabrics and metalware. By 1900 it was famed as a world leader in the Arts and Crafts

COMMODES & WASHSTANDS

The word 'commode' actually refers to French chests of drawers (see pp.62–63), but the polite Victorians also used it to describe what the Georgians called 'night tables': cupboards that held chamber pots.

Washstands vary from simple tripod stands (sometimes erroneously called 'wig stands') to small cabinets. They were made to hold wash basins and jugs, and usually have drawers for toiletries. Although, in common with commodes, washstands are no longer bought with their original use in mind, they can make attractive features in bedrooms, halls or drawing rooms.

▶ **DECORATION**
This late Georgian pine washstand has been repainted at a later date and looks very attractive. Beware,

however: replacing its missing bowl and jug could end up costing as much as the stand itself.
£250–350

▼ **CORNER COMMODES**
This mahogany-veneered corner

commode, made c.1810, was well shaped for its original purpose with its arm rests and back

support. Nowadays, it would probably be more useful as a TV cabinet.
£600–900

◀ **VICTORIAN WASHSTANDS**
In the Victorian era, large, marble-topped washstands were made *en suite* with other bedroom furniture. This is a fairly grand one that was made c.1870 from Oregon pine by Howard & Sons; you can, however, find more modestly priced examples.
£800–1,200

◀ **AUTHENTICITY**
Washstands are rarely faked, but signs of wear are always reassuring. You can see where the jug was placed on the stretcher of this typical corner washstand, made from mahogany c.1810.
£400–600

▶ **FAUX BAMBOO**
Imitation bamboo furniture made from beech was popular from the late 18th century onwards. With its wooden casters, this bedside cabinet, made c.1900, is typically French; English cabinets tend to have ceramic or brass casters.
£400–600

▶ **ALTERATIONS**
On this c.1830 solid-mahogany commode the lower serpentine part pulls out. The white ceramic casters are later additions from the Victorian period. Commodes have been altered more than any other form of furniture and they are rarely found as they were originally made. Many have had their lower parts converted to cupboards or drawers, but this does not affect prices unduly.
£500–700

GARDEN FURNITURE I

Eighteenth-century paintings sometimes show ladies and gentlemen outside with what would appear to be Georgian garden furniture. In fact, in the days of servants there was probably little difference between the furniture made for indoor use and that made for outdoor use. Purpose-built garden furniture was made, for the most part, from the Victorian era onwards as conservatories became increasingly popular.

Garden furniture changed dramatically after the improvement of iron casting, which was pioneered by the Coalbrookdale Iron Company in the 1840s. Garden furniture is very popular, and as values have risen, it has increasingly fallen prey to thieves.

COALBROOKDALE
Coalbrookdale of Ironbridge, Shropshire, the leading manufacturers in Britain of cast-iron garden furniture in the 19th century, made a popular range of ornately cast benches, tables and chairs. Many of the designs popularized at the Great Exhibition of 1851 were based on naturalistic forms such as nasturtiums, ivy, horse-chestnut leaves, ferns and oak leaves.

▲ RARITY
Coalbrookdale seats were listed in the company's catalogue and certain designs are less common and therefore more valuable than others. This Medallion pattern seat, produced c.1870, is one of the rarer examples. Original paint is almost impossible to find, but should always be kept if in acceptable condition.
£7,000–8,000

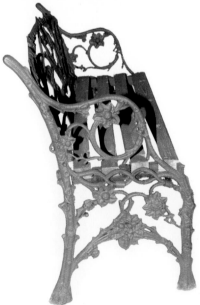

◀ SEATS
Cast-iron seating was fitted with metal, pine or oak slatted seats. This passion-flower cast-iron bench by Haywood of Derby, made c.1860, has had its slats replaced. This is a fairly common alteration that does not greatly affect value.
£1,500–3,000

BEWARE
The rising value of cast-iron furniture has led to many reproductions. This Gothic pattern seat, made in the 1990s, is a replica of an 1860s Coalbrookdale design. Some reproductions include the date of the 'original', but seek expert advice if you are in doubt.
£700–900

SIGNS OF AUTHENTICITY
● Crisp casting.
● Registration or 'kite' stamp – this may be indistinct even on a genuine piece.
● Foundry mark.

◀ **WOODEN FURNITURE**
This green-painted country chair dates from c.1830 and, although it is equally at home in the kitchen or the garden, it should always be stored indoors. Wooden painted furniture has little resilience to wet weather, and not much has survived.
£300–400 (painted; much less if stripped)

▲ **GARDEN SETS**
By the early 20th century, garden furniture such as this teak 1930s set became increasingly practical, if less elaborate. This sturdy set, with its six chairs, was cleverly designed to hold a parasol; note, too, that the chairs can be tucked under the table to keep them dry in wet weather.
£800–900

GARDEN FURNITURE II

The most expensive garden furniture is that made from marble or stone. Most marble furniture originated in Italy, but stone seats and benches were also carved from local materials by stonemasons throughout Europe. Coade stone, which is an early type of reconstituted stone made by a method that has been kept secret since the 18th century, is also extremely valuable. Among the more affordable garden furniture is a wide range of attractive, metal bent-wire pieces, produced in France at the beginning of the 20th century, that can often cost less than the modern equivalent. The market for 1940s metal dining tables and chairs is growing, and prices are rising.

BEWARE

Just because a piece looks weathered, it does not necessarily mean that it is old. You can achieve the moss-clad look in a matter of weeks if you paint a modern piece of stone furniture with sour milk! (Note that this will result in a decreased value.)

▲ MARBLE

Garden furniture made from Italian marble became extremely popular in the 19th century. It was bought by tourists in Italy as a souvenir and, later, as demand grew, widely exported for sale to other countries. Quality varies, and you can buy plain tables and benches for around £1,000. The attractive carving on this one raises its value.
£2,500–4,000

WHAT TO LOOK FOR

- Carrara marble statuary.
- Stone benches – these are less expensive but can be very attractive when they are weathered.
- Early types of reconstituted stone.
- Avoid modern stone or cement.

◀ **SPRUNG CHAIRS**
The flat, curving strips of metal that form the back and seat of this French chair create sprung supports that are much more comfortable to sit on than most metal seats. Made c.1900, the price of this one is reduced because it is in need of repair. In better condition it might cost half as much again. £60–80

▼ **VALUE**
A single, stylishly designed wire chair, such as this one made in France in the 1920s, would cost £30 to £40; a set of six would multiply the value and be worth between £300 and £400.

▲ **WIRE SETTEE**
This attractive and affordable French garden settee, produced c.1900, is made from industrial heavy-gauge wire, but there is a clever attention to detail in the way the tendrils weave in and out, lightening the overall effect. £300–400

▶ **CONDITION**
When you buy any type of metal furniture, make sure that the wire is strong – the welding is vulnerable to damage from rust. Metal garden furniture will last longer if you repaint it regularly and this does not reduce the value of less expensive pieces. £50–60

WICKER & BAMBOO

Wicker and bamboo are light and relatively inexpensive materials – this makes them ideal for conservatory and garden furniture that is frequently moved. Bamboo furniture with Oriental-style lacquer tops became extremely popular in the Edwardian period, and large numbers of inexpensive small tables were made in Japan for the Western market. Wicker furniture enjoyed a peak of popularity between 1920 and 1940. During this period the name Lloyd Loom became synonymous with an innovative type of wicker furniture made from twisted paper fibres that were reinforced with metal wire.

Bamboo furniture was popular during the Regency period, when it was used to furnish chinoiserie interiors. Beech was often carved in imitation of bamboo.

◀ BAMBOO TABLES
This bamboo tea table, with folding trays and lacquer top decorated in traditional colours, typifies the type of furniture made at the beginning of the 20th century. Few items of this type have survived in such good condition but, even so, it would not be very expensive.
£80–120

BEWARE
Lloyd Loom furniture is simple to identify. An ordinary magnet will enable you to tell if a chair was made by Lloyd Loom or if, like this example produced during the 1930s and 1940s, it was made from bamboo. A genuine piece contains metal wires within the upright strands, and this is why a magnet will stick to it.

▲ LLOYD LOOM
Lloyd Loom was the brainchild of the American Marshall B. Lloyd, who developed a method of producing furniture from bentwood frames covered in a machine-made, twisted paper fibre. Many different styles were manufactured but this design is probably the most famous. This example was manufactured c.1935 and is worth £60 to £80. Previously, wicker furniture was handmade from natural materials, such as cane and rattan, which were less robust and impossible to mass-produce.

▶ MODERN LLOYD LOOM

Modern furniture in classic Lloyd Loom styles is being produced today, but it is usually easy to identify. This is because all Lloyd Loom was originally marked with a label that varied according to the date of manufacture; many of the pieces were also date stamped. Labels are usually attached to the frame of seating, or to the underside of items such as linen baskets and tables.

LABELS

The Lusty company secured the franchise to produce Lloyd Loom furniture in England. This label was used between 1937 and 1940.

RANGE

A huge range of general household furniture was made by Lloyd Loom, including tables, linen baskets, dressing tables, chests and small cabinets.

CHILDREN'S FURNITURE I

Furniture made for children tends to follow the then current fashions prevailing for adult, full-sized furniture in scaled-down form. As you can see from the following pages, chairs were by far the most common pieces made for children.

Other items, such as baby walkers, chests, cribs, beds, bureaux and bookcases were also made, but they are less common and tend to command premiums for this reason. Quality children's furniture of the 17th and 18th centuries is much scarcer than the equivalent full-sized pieces and it is keenly collected. Prices, as a result, can be surprisingly high.

Children's furniture made in the 19th and early 20th centuries tends to be easier to find and is therefore much more affordable. Salesmen's samples are generally smaller and more elaborate than furniture that has been made for the nursery.

◀ COMMODES
The bobbin-turned legs and scroll-carved back on this late 17th-century beechwood potty chair are similar to the decoration that you would expect to see on the full-sized high-backed chairs of the same date.
£1,000–1,500

▼ COTS
Brass or cast-iron cots and cribs were popular in the late Victorian and Edwardian periods. This example from the late 19th century is very practical: it can easily be collapsed by pulling out the brass pins (a technique still used today by some crib makers).
£150–250

CRADLE STYLES
● Rockers on cradles from the 17th and 18th centuries are usually attached with pegs to the end posts; on later cradles the rockers are attached to the carcass.
● The sides on cradles made in the 17th century are usually panelled, but plain on those from the 18th century.

◀ MINIATURE BUREAUX
Although this appears to be an adult's desk, in fact, it measures only 20 in (50.8 cm) high. It is a rare example of a miniature bureau made for a child to use and play with. The exterior quality of this piece is similar to that of a full-sized version, but the interior is far less refined.
£1,000–1,500

WHAT TO LOOK FOR
It is important to distinguish between furniture designed for children to use, such as the 17th-century commode chair or the cot on the opposite page, and the more valuable miniature furniture made for children to play with. These miniatures are often erroneously called apprentice pieces; some may have been intended as samples.

DATING
Because children's furniture follows the same stylistic changes as full-sized pieces, you can usually date it in the same way. The ogee bracket feet on this bureau (above) point to a date of c.1750–1770.

▶ MINIATURE CHESTS
The heavy, turned columns on either side of this mahogany-veneered chest of drawers, produced about 1820, are typical of chests that were made in the north of England. As is the case with many pieces of miniature furniture, the proportions are slightly different. Note that the top drawer is much deeper than you would expect it to be on an adult version.
£800–1,200

CHILDREN'S FURNITURE II

From c.1800 onwards, an enormous variety of chairs was made especially for children. The Astley Cooper Correction Chair is one example: a late 18th-century chair that forced the sitter into an upright pose. Complex chairs with multiple uses were made as well: high chairs that could be separated to make chairs and play tables or folded into walkers.

Many extant pieces of children's furniture were made in the late Victorian and Edwardian periods for less affluent homes. Many later children's chairs are attractive and functional and can be found for modest sums. Sometimes the proportions of pieces made for children are not as well drawn as those of the full-size and miniature versions.

◀ WINDSORS
Children's Windsor chairs were made both as high chairs and as low chairs. This low chair (which was produced c.1800) shows the combination of woods found on full-sized Windsors: the back is yew, the seat elm, and the rails and legs are beech. The crinoline stretcher adds appeal and value. £800–1,000

▶ CHIPPENDALE CHAIRS
This is a modern reproduction, made in Mauritius, of a child's Chippendale chair. With a little wear, a buyer could be fooled into thinking that it was made in the 18th century. £100–200

▲ OTHER WINDSORS
Most early country furniture was painted, but, unfortunately, the paint has rarely survived. Do not strip paint even if it is wearing off; an old surface will raise a piece's value. This country piece could date from as broad a period as 1750 to 1850. It is worth between £500 and £1,000.

► REGENCY STYLES

Although this ebonized child's chair follows a Regency design, it was probably made about 1900. The value of this piece is greatly reduced because the frame has been crudely repainted. £50–70

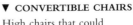

▼ CONVERTIBLE CHAIRS

High chairs that could change into go-carts or baby walkers (sometimes called 'metamorphic' chairs) were first made at the end of the 19th century. This one is adorned with what seems to be its original transfer. It probably dates from c.1930–1940 and is made from beech and plywood, and has cast-iron wheels. £60–80

► HIGH CHAIRS

Until the 19th century most high chairs were made to be pushed against tables, so they rarely have their own trays or restraining bars. High chairs usually relied on the arms to hold the child securely. This elm and beech 19th-century high chair is impossible to date accurately because it is based on the Mendlesham chairs made in East Anglia, which were common from c.1800 to 1900. £200–300

PINE KITCHEN FURNITURE I

From the late 18th century onwards, pine was either used for the backs, carcasses and drawer linings of pieces veneered with more expensive timbers, or for cheaper furniture that was then painted.

Much early pine kitchen furniture was actually built into a room. As the fashion for stripped pine grew in the 1960s, many pieces were removed from their original locations and converted into free-standing pieces.

It is rare to find a piece of pine furniture in its original condition; most has been adapted, stripped or converted to suit modern tastes. These pieces, however, can be just as valuable. Watch out for pine furniture that is made from old floorboards; it is worth buying, but do not pay the price of a genuine antique.

▶ **DRESSERS**
Made of 19th-century pine, this high dresser has been adapted to 20th-century use. The classical upper part of the dresser with its heavy pilasters is not reflected in the base, which is simpler in style. The eight-bottle wine-rack is a modern idea – an addition that would not be seen on early pieces.
£2,000–2,500

◀ **SIDE CABINETS**
This quirky side cabinet, made c.1900, could be mistaken for a table with cupboard doors added. Although the wood is rather stark and newly stripped, this is a utilitarian piece that with use and polish would develop patina and hold its value.
£300–400

► **FRENCH STYLE**
This side cabinet, with its elegantly panelled cupboard door, is reminiscent of French provincial furniture. Made c.1900, there would probably have been a deep plinth running around the base. The feet look as if they are fairly recent additions.
£300–400

◄ **SIDE TABLES**
Made during the last twenty years of the 19th century, this table would fit comfortably into a sitting-room, bedroom or kitchen. The drawer handles are later additions; turned wooden handles might be more in keeping with the piece's style.
£250–350

► **SMALLER PIECES**
As the fashion for country-style kitchens has grown, small pine 'kitchenware' has become increasingly difficult to find. This washboard is inexpensively made with a rudimentary frame and ribbed glass.
£50–75

WHAT TO LOOK FOR
Other small kitchen pieces you might find include:
● meat safes;
● plate racks;
● clothes airers;
● spoon racks.
Beware: plate racks and airers are in short supply and reproductions have been made.

PINE KITCHEN FURNITURE II

As with the pieces featured here, most pine furniture that you see today has been stripped of its original finish, although nearly all pine furniture was painted when first made. The techniques for decorating pine were often inventive and included scumble (softening the painted finish by applying an opaque top coat of a different shade), *faux* marbling, and graining to simulate expensive woods. In recent years there has been increased demand for old pine with its original painted finish and such pieces command a premium.

◄ **SETS OF CHAIRS**
This armchair, made during the mid-19th century, would be desirable on its own, but even more so if it was part of a set.

Individually, this chair would be worth £300 to £400, while a set of six chairs and two matching armchairs could fetch between £3,000 and £4,000.

► **LADDER-BACKS**
Rush-seated ladder-backs such as this one are another popular style of pine kitchen chair. A single chair is of relatively little value (it would sell for around £50), but as part of a set of six or more the same chair might be worth twice as much.

▲ **HIGH-BACK CHAIRS**
This is the most common style of high-back pine arm chair, constructed with a shaped, flat-slatted back and turned legs and stretchers.
£300–400

◀ **EXTENDING**
TABLES
On late Victorian and
Edwardian extending
tables such as this, the
winding mechanism is
usually reliable. Make
sure that the leaves are
original by comparing
the colour and grain
of the wood. Tables of
this design are likely
to be found in a more
sophisticated walnut or
mahogany. Pieces in
these woods will cost
50 per cent more than
those made in pine.
£1,000–1,500

▼ **KITCHEN TABLES**
Before buying a plank-
top table try sitting at it
first. A table with a
deep frieze, such as this
one, made c.1900, can
be uncomfortable if it

has been reduced in
height, particularly if
you are a tall person.
About 30in (76cm)
will be high enough to
suit most people.
£1,000–2,000

BEWARE
Check the joints of stripped pine furniture
very carefully for strength and firmness; if
the piece has been stripped in an acid bath,
any glued joints may be seriously weakened.

EARLY MIRRORS

Mirrors range from grand giltwood examples made in the 18th century that cost tens of thousands of pounds to composition mirrors and small dressing table mirrors that can cost less than modern reproductions. Early glass, or 'Vauxhall Plate' as it was known, was not made in big sheets, so large mirrors often had two or more pieces of mirrored glass butted together. All types of mirror are extremely popular with collectors, and there are specialist dealers who sell nothing but this type of furniture. Make sure that the mirror you buy is not simply a picture frame that has had a glass plate inserted.

◀ JAPANNED MIRRORS

This mirror frame, made c.1710, has been painted in the then fashionable Oriental style, a technique known as japanning. The shape of the mirror suggests that it was made to hang above a fireplace. The difference in tone of the panel of glass in the centre implies that it is a replacement; it is still worth between £2,500 and £4,000.

▼ GEORGIAN MIRRORS

Made c.1750, this small, well-made, mahogany-veneered mirror has been decorated with giltwood Prince of Wales feathers. Fakes of this style abound and prices have been kept low at £500 to £600. It can be difficult to identify a fake from the back (some even have old newspaper stuck on them) but the carving will be crudely under-cut, seeming flatter and somewhat naive, with a darker, more even appearance.

GEORGIAN UNDERCUTTING

The detail above, from the back of a Georgian carved giltwood mirror, shows how the back of the carved decoration was tapered inwards (undercut) so that the decoration appeared lighter when viewed from the front or side. Few later copies have such attention to detail. The accumulation of dirt that you can see here is also difficult to simulate and is a reassuring sign of age. Undercutting is a term that applies to all carving, whether on a mirror or the back of a chair splat.

◀ REGENCY CONVEX MIRRORS
The convex mirror first became fashionable in the early 19th century. This one dates from c.1820 and is the simplest type made; the grander versions are surmounted by eagles. These mirrors were also popular from the 1880s to the 1920s. The (not infallible) rule of thumb is that the smaller the mirror, the later it was produced. The gilding on this plain one is slightly chipped, but it would still be worth between £400 and £600; a later copy might cost £200 to £300.

▼ CHEVAL MIRRORS
By the 19th century, large plates of glass could be cast, and the free-standing mirror known as the horse (or cheval) glass became popular. 'Cheval' means horse in French, and the name given to the mirror refers to its four supporting legs. £800–1,000

▲ ROCOCO REVIVAL MIRRORS
This elaborate girandole (a mirror with candle sconces), one of a pair, is a product of the huge revival of everything rococo during the 1830s. Unlike a genuine rococo piece of the 1750s, the carving is not as light or attenuated, and the detail is too crowded and fussy. Even so, the quality and condition are impressive, and the pair would be worth £8,000 to £12,000.

LATER MIRRORS

Whenever possible, try to buy a mirror with its original glass. If your mirror's glass is unacceptably murky, it is preferable to have the glass re-silvered rather than to replace the glass completely. If the glass is cracked and you do have to replace it, try to find glass of an appropriate thickness. Bear in mind that heavy Victorian glass, especially when sharply bevelled, looks incongruous on a Georgian mirror.

▶ **DRESSING TABLE MIRRORS**

Shield-shaped mirrors are typical of Sheraton's and Hepplewhite's designs of the late 18th century. Dressing table mirrors, such as this one, made c.1780, were intended to stand on gentlemen's mahogany chests of drawers. They are not in vogue today and would represent good value at between £300 and £400.

DATING

A simple test with a coin can give you an idea of the age of the glass.

Georgian glass such as this is relatively thin, therefore the reflection of the coin appears quite close. The bevelling should be attractively shallow, while the cutting may be slightly uneven.

By the mid-19th century, glass was made much thicker, and therefore the reflection of the coin is noticeably further away. The bevelling is cut at a more acute angle, and there is no variation in cutting.

This is a modern imitation 'antique' glass, made in Italy. The impurities are regular, and the closeness of the coin's reflection shows the glass to be even thinner than that made in the 18th century.

COMPOSITION

Less expensive mirrors were made from Victorian times onwards with plaster that had been reinforced with wire – this was known as 'composition'. The damage to this mirror, made c.1860, reveals the vulnerability of plaster to breakage. Composition frames remain much less expensive than giltwood versions and you should not buy a damaged one.

▲ REPRODUCTIONS

Although described in a catalogue as '19th-century', this is more likely a 20th-century continental version of a George III-style mirror. Copies such as this one can be bought at auction for very reasonable prices.
£400–600

◀ CONDITION

The glass in this 1890s mirror is quite badly discoloured. You can see the skeleton of the mirror's under-frame in the glass where the back of the mirror has been exposed to a damp wall. This sort of damage presents a dilemma, but the best advice would be not to replace the glass.
£700–1,000

◀ VENETIAN MIRRORS

Mirrors such as this one were first produced in Venice's glass-making district, Murano, in the late 19th century; they are still being made there today. This one probably dates from c.1900 and is worth £1000 to £1500.

A modern one would fetch less at auction, but it would be far more expensive to buy new. Be sure to check the dating given in the auction catalogue – only some reveal that such pieces are modern. If in doubt, check with the expert in charge of the sale.

SCREENS

Folding screens were originally made as practical objects to help prevent drafts. Oriental lacquer, papier mâché, leather and wood with embroidered or textile panels are among the wide range of materials used for screens. Their value lies chiefly in their decorative appeal rather than their age and original embroidery will raise prices.

Fire-screens and pole-screens were used to protect the occupants of a room from the direct heat of roaring fires. Modern central heating and smaller rooms mean that they are no longer of huge practical use, but they are still attractive in front of fireplaces. Tripod screens from the 18th century with their original embroidery are much sought after.

◀ **EMBROIDERED SCREENS**
This good-quality screen, made c.1860 from giltwood with embroidered silk panels, has five folds – most have only three or four. It is in good condition and has ceramic casters that allow it to be pulled out easily and elaborate hinges that enable its sections to fold either way.
£1,000–1,500

▶ **POLE-SCREENS**
At a time when much make-up was made from wax and melted if it became too warm, pole-screens protected a lady's face from the heat of open fires. This elaborate pole-screen, made c.1845, painted and gilded, and inset with a tapestry panel in imitation of French rococo styles, is worth £1,000 to £2,000.

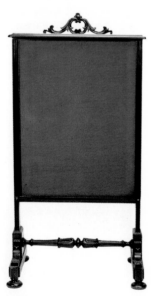

◀ **FIRE-SCREENS**
The value of this solid-mahogany c.1835 fire-screen is reduced because it needs re-upholstering. As with many fire-screens of this type, it has a hidden slide in the top that pulls out to give additional protection from the heat of the fire.
£250–400

BEWARE

Because pole-screens are no longer in demand, they are often made into tilt-top tables. The base of this table belonged to an 18th-century pole-screen; the top was added during the 19th century. £1,000–1,500

▼ RANGE OF MATERIALS

Fire-screens were made from a wide range of materials; this one, made c.1865, has a simulated bamboo frame and a carefully embroidered filigree panel in the centre. It is of very high quality and may have been the work of Howard & Sons. £500–1,000

► LATER SCREENS

Screens decorated in the Oriental style continued to be fashionable until the beginning of World War I. This four-fold screen, typically painted with Chinoiserie-style birds, flowers and butterflies, is in rather worn condition but decorative enough for this not to matter greatly. £2,000–3,000

CANTERBURIES

The furniture designer Thomas Sheraton named these popular music stands after the first person to order one from him: the Archbishop of Canterbury. First made in 1803, canterburies were originally intended to hold books or sheet music; today, they make perfect magazine racks. Canterburies have always been popular pieces of furniture and hold their value well.

▶ **DATING**
The proportions of a canterbury can give an important clue to its date. Earlier examples were larger but lighter than later ones, such as this one, which was made c.1820. This piece has lost a caster, which means that a repair is essential; this will not necessarily have a significant effect on the value.
£800–1,200

◀ **ALTERATIONS**
Check carefully for signs of tampering. This piece of furniture seems to be the base of an *étagère*; dividers made from stained plywood have been added to turn it into a 'canterbury'. This makes it of little value.
£200–250

WHAT TO LOOK FOR
● Original cross bars and supports.
● Original casters on the feet.
● A drawer is a definite bonus.

▶ **VARIATIONS**
This is not a typical piece: the legs, which have luckily survived intact, are higher than usual and there is only one divider running from front to back.
£2,000–3,000

WHATNOTS & DUMB WAITERS

Dumb waiters, which were made for dining-rooms from c.1750 onwards, were used for displaying food when the servants had been dismissed and the gentlemen tucked into their port. Whatnots and *étagères* became popular in the last years of the 18th century. Both are types of stand and both have open shelves, but *étagères* are somewhat wider and larger than whatnots. Victorian *étagères* with fret-cut decorations are much sought after.

◀ DUMB WAITERS
This classic mahogany dumb waiter of c.1750 is especially interesting. Underneath one of the trays there is an old label showing that it once belonged to the Earl of Shannon. An illustrious provenance always adds cachet to a piece and makes it more sought after.
£1,500–2,500

You should never remove old labels from a piece of furniture; they are fascinating proof of its history.

▼ ETAGERES
Etagères – or, as they are sometimes called, 'serving tables' – were originally employed in the dining-room for displaying bowls of food. Some examples of *étagère* feature complex collapsing mechanisms that allow them to be folded flat into tables. Note that this mahogany *étagère*, made about 1830, has unusual marble inset shelves.
£1,800–2,200

▲ WHATNOTS
The turned pillars of this early Victorian rosewood whatnot, made c.1840, are a nod to late 17th-century styles. Whatnots are useful nowadays for displaying objects or for stereos, so they are always in demand.
£600–900

STEPS & STANDS

As you can see from the diverse range of objects featured here, the range of collectable smaller furniture is extremely varied. The value of a piece will depend, as always, on a combination of its quality, decorative appeal and condition.

If you are thinking of buying a piece with moving parts, or with a complex opening and closing mechanism, make sure that no parts are missing. If there is a part missing, or if the mechanism has been damaged in any way, it may prove expensive to restore.

▼ BED STEPS
Bed steps were used to help weary or short people into their high beds; sometimes they doubled as commodes and contained small cupboards for chamber pots. This standard set, produced about 1840, is made of mahogany and has leather-lined treads.
£700–1,000

▲ BOOK STANDS
Book stands are among a number of smaller pieces that were made for libraries from the mid-18th century. Designs vary, but all have raised surfaces, often adjustable, to support books. This one, made by Howard & Son c.1870 from Oregon pine, has a telescopic stem that adds to its value.
£800–1,200

▶ ARCHITECTS' TABLES
This architect's table, which was built c.1760, has a hinged top, and an apron that pulls forward to form a writing surface; there are two drawers and a leather slide beneath. This example is made of walnut; most are made of mahogany.
£5,000–7,000

SHELVES & DRINKS TABLES

Small hanging shelves and racks date from the 17th century and earlier, and were used both for display and storage. Tables and trolleys for drinks usually date from the late Victorian and Edwardian periods (c.1890 to 1920). They were popular in more affluent households because they could be moved about easily from room to room and locked away from thirsty servants!

▶ **SPOON RACKS**
Spoon racks are typically made from oak or country woods and, although usually fairly simple in their design, can be very decorative. This one, made c.1780, has an open compartment in the base that probably held candles.
£300–500

▼ **DRINKS TROLLEYS**
This late 19th-century beech drinks trolley would have been perfect for wheeling drinks into the garden.

The top is a removable glass-lined tray, and the shelves below are also glass, which is more practical than wood in the event of a spillage.
£400–600

▲ **WALL SHELVES**
Delicate fretwork, as seen on the sides and galleries of this wall shelf, is susceptible to damage. Sadly, the fact that this decorative 19th-century example is slightly the worse for wear reduces its price significantly.
£1,000–1,500

◀ **DRINKS TABLES**
This mahogany drinks table by Thornhill, c.1900, opens to reveal a selection of glasses and three decanters in a locking tantalus. The 'tantalus' is named after the mythical Ancient Greek king who was forced to stand surrounded by tempting water that receded when he tried to drink it.
£1,000–1,500

TRAYS, BUCKETS & BOXES

The wide range of smaller 18th- and 19th-century antiques for the dining-room are often beautifully made and highly sought after for their decorative appeal. Although, generally, these pieces are no longer used for their original purposes, they are surprisingly adaptable to modern life. A butler's tray makes a good side table, while a knife box can be useful for stationery and a bucket can serve as a waste basket.

▼ BUTLERS' TRAYS

The detachable top of a butler's tray allowed it to be used both as an occasional table and for carrying food and crockery to and from the kitchen. Few stands are found complete with their original trays. This one has a reproduction top and a stand that was made c.1880. £300–500

▼ BUCKETS

Mahogany buckets with copper or brass banding were used in the 18th and 19th centuries to carry plates (in which case there is a gap down most of one side) or, as with this 19th-century example, for carrying logs, coal and peat. £400–600

▶ KNIFE BOXES

Wooden boxes, such as this one made c.1750–60, would typically have stood one on either end of a sideboard, while the interiors would have been fitted for cutlery. As with most boxes, this one has been converted for stationery; the shell inlay is also a later addition, perhaps covering up a crest. Wooden urns with lids were also fitted for cutlery in the 18th century. Pairs of these are very decorative and often extremely valuable. Some examples may fetch as much as £2,000 each. A pair of wooden knife boxes in the same style as this one would be fetch between £2,000 and £3,000.

CELLARETS & TEAPOYS

Cellarets and wine coolers were used for the short-term storage of wine in the dining-room and normally stood beneath or to the side of the sideboard. Cellarets usually have locking lids and are sometimes lead-lined with a plug in the base to drain away melted ice. Wine coolers, or cisterns, were not lined until c.1730 and were mostly used for red wine. By the end of the 18th century the terms 'cellaret' and 'wine cooler' were largely interchangeable. Sarcophagus-shaped cellarets from the early 19th century are desirable.

Teapoys were used in the drawing-room for the storage and mixing of tea. Because tea was expensive, teapoys were well made and usually fitted with good-quality locks.

▶ **STYLES**
The low sarcophagus-shaped wine cooler was popular in the Regency and early Victorian periods in the 19th century. This mahogany example is fairly plain, apart from its attractively carved leaf-scroll legs. Grander wine coolers have applied mounts and carved details that add value.
£1,200–1,800

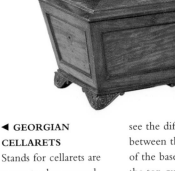

◀ **GEORGIAN CELLARETS**
Stands for cellarets are prone to damage and often replaced, as is the case with this classic oval mahogany example, made c.1770. You can see the difference between the colour of the base and that of the top quite clearly, and this reduces the value of the piece quite considerably.
£1,500–2,000

▶ **TEAPOYS**
This flame-figured mahogany teapoy of c.1830 has several features of quality:
● zinc-lined caddies that fit perfectly;
● heavy cut-glass mixing bowls that are still intact;
● a lock by a premier maker: Bramah;
● a Gillow stamp – this can add 30 per cent to the value.
£1,000–1,500

20TH-CENTURY DESIGNERS I

Great changes in furniture design occurred during the 20th century as new manufacturing techniques and materials were introduced. Many of the leading designers such as Marcel Breuer, Ludwig Mies van der Rohe and Le Corbusier were also established avant-garde architects. Their furniture was tailor-made for modern homes, where space was often at a premium, so folding and stacking furniture features prominently.

Much 20th-century furniture was designed to be mass-produced, rather than handmade by craftsmen in the 18th-century tradition.

Novel, inexpensive materials, such as tubular steel and moulded plywood, were used in simple and streamlined forms, with minimal surface decoration.

From the second half of the century onwards the availability of plastics and fibreglass allowed designers to go beyond the purity and precision of the machine aesthetic and produce biomorphic shapes and organic designs – almost any concept, no matter how bizarre, could be realized. At last designers were able to break away from derivative forms and invent new styles of furniture.

◀ **CHARLES EAMES**
The American designer Charles Eames originally designed this moulded, rosewood-veneered plywood and leather-upholstered lounge chair and ottoman (designs '670' and '671') as a television chair for the playwright Billy Wilder. The set was commercially produced by the American manufacturer Herman Miller in 1956; usually upholstered in black (less often in tan and only rarely in white), it is still being reproduced today. Miller originals are worth £1,000 to £1,200; reproductions, oddly, fetch between £2,500 and £3,000.

UPHOLSTERY
- The original upholstery is always desirable – but not always practical.
- Re-upholstering carried out by the original manufacturer will not affect value and is a good selling point.
- Black or dark blue leather is usually more desirable than tan.
- White upholstery is particularly rare.

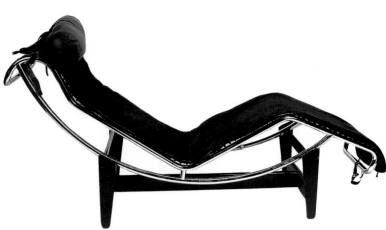

◄ **LE CORBUSIER**
The French architect
Le Corbusier designed
this tubular-steel *chaise
longue* with Pierre
Jeanneret and Charlotte
Perriand in 1928. It
was made in very
limited numbers by
Thonet Frères, Paris.
In the 1960s and 1970s
it was reissued by the
firm Cassina, and most
of those for sale today,
at £700 to £1,000,
date from this period.
New pieces by Palazetti
cost about £800.

► **GRAND COMFORT**
From a 1928 design by
Le Corbusier, Pierre
Jeanneret and Charlotte
Perriand, this tubular-
steel and leather chair
was originally made by
Thonet Frères and later
by Heidi Weber (1959)
and Cassina (1965). A
new version costs more
than a 1960s chair, at
£600 to £1,000.

◄ **SOFT PAD CHAIRS**
These chairs were
originally designed by
Charles Eames in
1958 as part of his
Outdoor Series.
Herman Miller
produced a version
intended for luxurious
offices in 1969; the
design is still produced.
A vintage high-back
example (right) would
sell for £600 to £900;
a side-arm chair (left) is
worth £300 to £400.

20TH-CENTURY DESIGNERS II

There seems little doubt that 20th-century furniture is one of the most promising collecting areas of the future. In recent years it has risen steadily in popularity in the UK, in continental Europe and in the USA. Auctions that are devoted to this field are now held by Bonhams and Christie's South Kensington. To capitalize on this market you will need to collect with care – look out for innovative designs that are attributable to recognized designers.

Remember that designs tend to be more collectable once they have gone out of production. If you are tempted to purchase a design that is still being produced, always try to find a vintage example – it might be cheaper now but you will find that it turns out to be the more valuable collector's item.

There is a booming cottage industry in 1990s Britain, with many young designers and craftsmen making innovative furniture for home and international markets.

▶ **MAURICE CALKA**
The biomorphic 'Boomerang Desk', by the French sculptor Maurice Calka, came in three variations; the design won the Grand Prix de Rome in 1969. The desk was one of the icons of late 1960s furniture and because it was only ever made in limited numbers it is extremely collectable.
£5,500–7,500

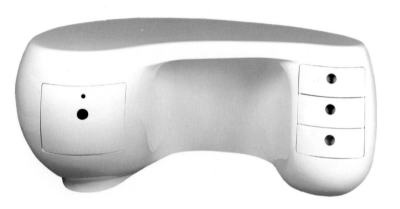

NAMES TO LOOK OUT FOR
- Alvar Aalto (Finland)
- Harry Bertoia (United States)
- Wendell Castle (United States)
- Arne Jacobsen (Denmark)
- Pierre Paulin (France)
- Ernest Race (England)
- Marcel Breuer (Germany)

◀ **VERNER PANTON**
The innovative Danish designer, Verner Panton, dreamt up this sculpture for the 'What is Design' exhibition held at the Louvre, Paris, in 1969.

The 12ft (364cm) high 'Living Tower' seat took four people: one on top, two on the projecting limbs, and one reclining on the bottom!
£3,500–5,500

◀ JASON CHAIRS

Designed by Carl Jacobs, another leading Danish designer, 'Jason Chairs' were designed to stack easily and were produced commercially by Kandya Ltd in the 1950s. Most were made in naturally coloured laminated wood; the painted finish on the examples seen here is rarer. £50–60 (each)

▼ HARP CHAIRS

20th-century designers have concentrated on seating far more than on other types of furniture; in modern homes the storage cupboards and shelving tend to be built in. The 'Harp' chair is a unusual and surprisingly comfortable seat, designed by Jorgen Hovelskov of Denmark in 1958. £200–300

◀ JOE COLUMBO

Italian designer Joe Columbo's furniture is notable for its elegant use of plastics, and his designs reflect his concept of a Utopian environment. 'Elda', this extravagantly upholstered lounge chair, was designed for the manufacturers Comfort in 1963. £400–600

▶ TULIP CHAIRS

Sculptural tulip chairs and matching tables were designed by the American designer Eero Saarinen in 1956. They were made by Knoll with moulded fibreglass seats and slender aluminium pedestal bases. £40–50

PART 5

INFORMATION

WHERE TO BUY

MAJOR AUCTION HOUSES

Biddle & Webb
Ladywood,
Middleway,
Birmingham,
West Midlands

Bonhams
Montpelier Street,
Knightsbridge,
London SW7

Bonhams
65–69 Lots Road,
London SW10

Christie's
8 King Street,
St James's,
London SW1

Christie's South Kensington
85 Old Brompton Road,
London SW7

Dreweatt & Neate
Donnington Priory,
Donnington,
Newbury,
Berkshire

Henry Spencer & Son
20 The Square,
Retford,
Nottinghamshire

Lawrence
South Street,
Crewkerne,
Somerset

Lots Road Auction Galleries
71 Lots Road,
London SW10

Mallams
Bocardo House,
St Michael's Street,
Oxford,
Oxfordshire

Outhwaite & Litherland
Kingsway Galleries,
Fontenoy Street,
Liverpool,
Merseyside

Phillips
Blenstock House,
101 New Bond Street,
London W1

Rosebery's
The Old Railway Booking Hall,
Crystal Palace,
Station Road,
London SE19

Russel Balwin & Bright
Ryelands Road,
Leominster,
Herefordshire

Sotheby's
34–35 New Bond Street,
London W1

Sotheby's Sussex
Summers Place,
Billingshurst,
West Sussex

Woolley & Wallis
Castle Street,
Salisbury,
Wiltshire

MAJOR ANTIQUES FAIRS

JANUARY

Dorchester Antiques Fair
Dorchester Hotel,
Park Lane,
Mayfair,
London W1

West London Antiques Fair
Kensington Town Hall,
Thornton Street,
London W8

Antiques Fair
Alexandra Palace,
Wood Green,
London N22

Decorative Antiques & Textiles Fair
King's College,
London SW3

LAPADA Antiques & Fine Art Fair
National Exhibition Centre,
Birmingham,
West Midlands

Antiques Fair
Palais de Beaux Arts,
10 rue Royal,
Brussels,
Belgium

Northern Antiques Fair
The Showground,
Harrogate,
North Yorkshire

The Annual Winter Antiques Show
7th Regiment Armory,
New York,
USA

FEBRUARY

Fine Art & Antiques Fair
Olympia,
London W14

Chester Antiques Show
The County Grandstand,
Chester Racecourse,
Cheshire

Harrogate Antiques & Fine Art Fair
The Royal Bath Assembly Rooms,
Harrogate,
North Yorkshire

Kenilworth Antiques Dealers' Fair
Chesford Grange,
Kenilworth,
Warwickshire

MARCH

The Chelsea Antiques Fair
Chelsea Old Town Hall,
King's Road,
London SW3

The Bath Decorative & Antiques Fair
The Pavilion,
Bath,
Avon

The European Fine Art Fair
MECC,
Maastricht,
The Netherlands

Decorative Antiques and Textiles Fair
King's College,
London SW3

APRIL

British International Antiques Fair
National Exhibition Centre,
Birmingham

Thames Valley Antiques Dealers' Association
School Hall,
Eton College,
Eton,
Berkshire

MAY
Buxton
Antiques Fair
The Octagon,
The Pavilion Gardens,
Buxton,
Derbyshire
BADA Fair
Duke of York's
Headquarters,
Chelsea,
London SW3

JUNE
The Fine Art &
Antiques Fair
Olympia,
London W14
The Grosvenor
House Art &
Antiques Fair
Grosvenor House
Hotel,
Park Lane,
London W1

JULY
South of England
Show
Ardingly,
Sussex

AUGUST
National Exhibition
Centre August Fair
Birmingham,
West Midlands
West London
Antiques Fair
Kensington
Town Hall,
Hornton Street,
Kensington,
London W8

SEPTEMBER
Chelsea
Antiques Fair

Chelsea Old
Town Hall,
King's Road,
London SW3
City Antiques &
Fine Art Fair
The Business
Design Centre,
London N1

OCTOBER
LAPADA
Antiques Fair
The Royal College
of Art,
Kensington Gore,
London SW7
The PAN Antiques
Fair
The Park Hall,
Amsterdam,
The Netherlands

NOVEMBER
The Fine Art &
Antiques Fair
Olympia,
London W14

DECEMBER
Westminster
Antiques Fair
Royal
Horticultural Hall,
Vincent Square,
London SW1

ANTIQUES
MARKETS
& CENTRES

BATH
Bath Antique Market
Guinea Lane,
Landsdown Road,
Bath,
Avon
(Wednesday)

BIRMINGHAM
Holliday Wharf
Antiques Centre
164 Holliday Street,
Birmingham,
West Midlands

DERBYSHIRE
Bakewell
Antiques Centre
King Street,
Bakewell,
Derbyshire

HERTFORDSHIRE
Herts & Essex
Antiques Centre
The Maltings,
Station Road,
Sawbridgeworth,
Hertfordshire

LONDON
Alfie's Antiques
Market
13–25 Church Street,
Off Edgware Road,
London NW8
(Tuesday to
Saturday)
Antiquarius
King's Road,
Chelsea,
London SW3
Bermondsey Market
Bermondsey Street,
Bermondsey,
London SE1
(Friday)
Camden Passsage
Islington,
London N1
(Wednesday
& Saturday)
Chenil Galleries
181 King's Road,
Chelsea,
London SW3

Grays Antiques
Market
Davis Street,
London W1
Portobello
Road Market
Portobello Road,
London W11
(Saturday)

LINCOLNSHIRE
Helmswell Antiques
Centres
Caenby Corner
Estate,
Helmswell Cliff,
Gainsborough,
Lincolnshire

NOTTINGHAMSHIRE
Portland Street
Antiques Centre
27 Portland Street,
Newark,
Nottinghamshire

OXFORDSHIRE
The Swan At
Tetsworth
High Street,
Tetsworth,
Oxfordshire

WHERE TO SEE

Visiting major collections in museums and houses open to the public is an invaluable way to learn about furniture. Listed below are some of the most noteworthy places to visit in Great Britain and Ireland.

Arlington Court
Arlington,
Nr Barnstaple,
Devon

Ascott
Wing,
Leighton Buzzard,
Hertfordshire

Ashdown House
Lambourn,
Newbury,
Berkshire

Attingham Park
Shrewsbury,
Shropshire

Audley End
Saffron Walden,
Essex

Bantry House
Bantry,
Co. Cork,
Ireland

Basildon Park
Lower Basildon,
Reading,
Berkshire

Belton House
Grantham,
Lincolnshire

Berrington Hall
Nr Leominster,
Hereford,
Herfordshire

Blenheim Palace
Woodstock,
Oxforshire

Blickling Hall
Blickling,
Norwich,
Norfolk

Bradley
Newton Abbot,
Devon

Braemar Castle
Brawmar,
Ballater,
Grampian

Broughton House
Banbury,
Oxfordshire

Burghley House
Stamford,
Northants

Calke Abbey
Ticknall,
Derby,
Derbyshire

Castle Howard
York,
North Yorkshire

Chatsworth
Bakewell,
Derbyshire

Clandon Park
West Clandon,

Guildford,
Surrey

Claydon House
Middle Claydon,
Nr Buckingham,
Buckinghamshire

Cothele
St Dominick,
Saltash,
Cornwall

Dunham Massey
Altrincham,
Cheshire

Felbrigg Hall
Norwich,
Norfolk

Fenton House
Windmill Hill,
Hampstead,
London NW3

Geffrye Museum
Kingsland Road,
Hackney,
London E2

Grantham House
Castlegate,
Grantham,
Lincolnshire

Greyfriars
Worcester,
Worcestershire

Gunby Hall
Gunby,
Lincolnshire

Haddon Hall
Bakewell,
Derbyshire

Ham House
Ham,
Richmond,
Surrey

Hampton Court Palace
Hampton,
Middlesex

Hardwick Hall
Doe Lea,
Chesterfield,
Derby

Harewood House
Leeds,
West Yorkshire

Hatfield House
Hatfield,
Hertfordshire

Holyroodhouse
(Palace of)
Abbey Strand,
Edinburgh

Hintner Ampner
Nr Alresford,
Hampshire

Houghton Hall
Houghton,
Norfolk

Hughendon Manor
High Wycombe,
Hertfordshire

Ickworth
Ickworth,
The Rotunda,
Horringer,
Bury St Edmunds,
Suffolk

Ightham Mote
Ivy Hatch,
Sevenoaks,
Kent

Kedleston Hall
Derby,
Derbyshire

Kensington Palace
Kensington,
London W8

Knebworth House
Knebworth,
Hertfordshire

Knightshayes Court
Bolham,
Tiverton,
Devon

Knole
Sevenoaks,
Kent

Lady Lever Art Gallery
Port Sunlight,
Wirral,
Merseyside

Longleat House
Warminster,
Wiltshire

Loughwood Meeting House
Dalwood,
Devon

Luton Hoo
Luton,
Bedfordshire

Malahide Castle
Malahide,

Co. Dublin,
Ireland

Montacute House
Montacute,
Somerset

Ormesby Hall
Ormesby,
Middlesbrough,
Cleveland

Osterley Park
Osterley,
Isleworth,
Middlesex

Owlette
Cobham,
Gravesend,
Kent

Oxburgh Hall
Oxborough,
Nr Kings's Lynn,
Norfolk

Parham House
Pulborough,
West Sussex

Petworth House
Petworth,
West Sussex

Polesden Lacey
Dorking,
Surrey

Royal Pavilion
The Old Steine,
Brighton,
East Sussex

Rufford Old Hall
Rufford,
Ormskirk,
Lancashire

Saltram
Plympton,
Plymouth,
Devon

Shugborough
Milford,
Nr Stafford,
Staffordshire

Southside House
Wimbledon
Common,
London SW19

Standen
East Grinstead,
East Sussex

Syon House
Isleworth,
Middlesex

Sizergh Castle
Sizergh,
Nr Kendal,
Cumbria

Sutton House
2 & 4 Homerton
High Street,
Hackney,
London E9

Tatton Park
Knutsford,
Cheshire

Tattershall Castle
Tattershall,
Lincoln,
Lincolnshire

Temple Newsam House
Leeds,
West Yorkshire

Trerice
Nr Newquay,
Cornwall

Uppark
South Harting,
Petersfield,
Hampshire

Victoria & Albert Museum
Cromwell Road,
London SW7

The Vyne
Sherbourne St John,
Basingstoke,
Hampshire

Waddesdon Manor
Aylesbury,
Buckinghamshire

Wallace Collection
Hertford House,
Manchester Square,
London W1

Wallington
Cambo,
Northumberland

Wilton House
Nr Salisbury,
Wiltshire

Wimpole Hall
Arrington,
Cambridgeshire

Windsor Castle
Windsor,
Berkshire

Woburn Abbey
Woburn,
Bedfordshire

GLOSSARY

Acanthus Leaf motif, originating in Classical architecture, used in carved decoration and metal mounts.

Ambulante Small portable pieces of French furniture.

Amphora Two-handled jar used originally in Classical antiquity.

Anthemion Floral motif resembling a honeysuckle flower, originating in Ancient Greek architecture.

Apron Concealing skirt of wood running beneath the seat-rail of chairs and sofas or between the drawers and legs of case furniture and dressers-on-stands.

Armada chest Chest for storing valuables from the 16th century; usually has metal bandings and an elaborate lock.

Armoire French tall cupboard with one or two doors.

Astragal A convex moulding, usually of wood, used for glazing bars on cabinet.

Bachelor's chest Chest of drawers with a hinged top that can be supported on lopers and opens to form a larger surface.

Backboard The wood (often unpolished) used to infill the back of furniture made to stand or hang against a wall.

Backstool A rudimentary form of chair made in the 16th century.

Ball foot Orb-shaped style used for the feet of chests of drawers.

Ball and claw Popular style for feet on chairs etc., depicting a taloned bird or animal foot clasping a ball.

Baluster turned A bulbous pillar – a form commonly seen on the legs of chairs and tables, and on pedestal supports.

Banding Strips of veneer laid around the edge of drawer fronts and the tops of tables and case furniture.

Barley twist Spiral turned pillars popular on chairs and tables in the late 17th century.

Belle Epoque Translated from French, it means 'beautiful period' and relates to the lavish styles of the late 19th century to World War I.

Bergère A French wing armchair or a chair in a similar style with caned or upholstered sides.

Birdcage support Hinged mechanism with small posts supporting two platforms, used on the top of a pedestal support to allow tripod tables to swivel.

Bombé Bulbous curving shape favoured particularly in continental Europe for commodes and other types of case furniture.

Bonheur du jour Small lady's writing cabinet, originated in France c.1760, popular in the 19th century in France and England.

Boulle marquetry Inlaid tortoiseshell or horn with metal (usually brass), developed in late 17th-century France by designer André Charles Boulle.

Bow front Convex form on chests of drawers from the late 18th century.

Bracket foot An 18th-century flat, shaped foot that extends diagonally from the floor to the carcass on the front and sides of case furniture.

Breakfront Furniture with a prominent central section, commonly seen on large bookcases and sideboards.

Broken pediment A pediment, or triangular superstructure, in which the central apex is absent and often filled with a carved motif, common on bureau bookcases, bookcases etc.

Brushing slide Retractable wooden board, found beneath the top and above the drawers of chests.

Bun foot Similar to a ball foot but more squashed, common on late 17th-century case furniture.

Bureau Sloping, fall-fronted writing desk, with drawers.

Bureau bookcase A bureau with a glazed bookcase.

Bureau plat French term for a writing table.

Burr Finely knotted grain commonly seen on veneers cut

from the base of
a tree.

Cabriole leg The
outwardly curving,
elongated S-shape
leg that became
popular for chairs
etc. from the late
17th century.

Canted corner
A chamfered or
bevelled corner
used as a decorative
feature on 18th-
century case
furniture.

Canterbury A rack
for holding music.

Cartouche
Decorative feature
resembling a scroll
of parchment with
curled edges.

Caryatid A female
figure of Ancient
Greek origin used
as an architectural
support; they
sometimes form
the supports on a
cabinet base.

Case furniture
Furniture made to
hold and store
objects, such as
chests, coffers and
cupboards.

Casters Small wheels
usually made from
brass, wood or
ceramic on the
base of chairs etc.,
which allow the
chair to be moved.

Cellaret Container
used from the 18th
century onwards
for storing and

cooling wine,
sometimes in
a sideboard.

Chaise longue
Upholstered chair
with an elongated
seat to support the
legs in a horizontal
upright position.

Chesterfield A
sprung upholstered
sofa, usually
buttoned, popular
in the late 19th
century.

Chiffonier Side
cabinet with
cupboards and
drawers below and
one or more low
shelves above.

Chinoiserie
Oriental-style
decoration popular
from the late 17th
century onwards.

Cleated ends The
tops of trestle and
refectory tables
made from several
long planks were
often secured at
each end by a strip
of wood with the
grain at a right
angle to the top.

Cock beading
Curved strip of
moulding often
applied to finish
edges of drawers.

Coffer Chest with a
hinged lid.

Commode An
elaborate chest of
drawers, popular
on the Continent;
in Victorian times

the term was used
to describe a small
cupboard to store
the chamber pot.

Composition
A man-made
malleable substance
commonly used to
make less expensive
mirror frames.

Console table
A table made to
stand against a wall
between windows,
usually with no
back support.

Corner cupboard
Hanging, low or
full-length cupboard,
of triangular form,
made to fit in a
corner, and usually
containing shelves
behind panelled or
glazed doors.

Credenza A popular
form of Victorian
side cabinet, often
with a combination
of glazed doors and
blind doors and
highly elaborately
decorated.

Cresting Carved
decoration found
on the highest
part of a piece
of furniture.

Crinoline stretcher
A curved stretcher
commonly found
on early types of
Windsor chairs.

Crocket Stylized,
protruding carved
leaf or flower motif
of architectural
origin, commonly

seen on Gothic-
style furniture.

Crossbanding
A veneered edge
made from strips
cut at right angles
to the main veneer.

Cup and cover
Bulbous form of
carved decoration
resembling an acorn,
found on Elizabethan
and early 17th-
century furniture.

Davenport Small
free-standing
writing desk
popular in the
Regency period,
with a hinged top
above a case of
side drawers.

Dentils Small
rectangular blocks
inspired by Ancient
architecture used to
form cornices
and mouldings.

Distressed A
piece of furniture
that has been
artificially aged.

Dovetails Spreading
wedge-shaped tenons
that interlock in
shaped mortises to
form a joint.

Dowel Small round
wooden peg used
to hold early
mortise and tenon
joints in place.

Drop-in seat
Upholstered seat
supported within
the frame of a
chair, but not
attached to it.

Drop handle
Tear-drop-shaped
handle commonly
seen on late 17th/
early 18th-century
furniture.

Drop leaf A table
with hinged flaps
that can be raised
when required.

Drum table Circular
writing table with
drawers in the
frieze and a
central pedestal.

Dummy board
Painted two-
dimensional cut-
out figure or
animal. Possibly
originally made
as fire-screens,
they were chiefly
for decorative
purposes.

Dummy drawer
A false drawer front
that looks like a
drawer.

Ebonized Wood
stained and painted
black to resemble
ebony.

Encoignure The
French term for a
corner cupboard.

Escritoire
Fall-fronted
writing desk with
a fitted interior.

Escutcheon Brass
plate surrounding
a keyhole.

Fall front The
hinged flap of a
writing desk that
pulls down to make
a writing surface.

Fauteuil A French
or French-style
upholstered
armchair.

Faux bois French
term meaning
wood painted to
resemble a more
exotic timber.

Featherbanding
Strips of veneer
around the edge
of a surface, cut
diagonally to the
main veneer.

Fielded panel
A raised panel
bordered by a
bevelled edge.

Figuring The
pattern made by
the grain of wood.

Finial A decorative
turned or carved
ornament.

Flame figuring
A veneer cut to
enhance the grain
of the wood and
resembling flames.

Fluting Concave
parallel furrows
used to decorate
columns, pilasters
or legs of chairs.

Fretwork Carved
geometric
decoration that
may be pierced or
blind and is used
as a border, or to
form a gallery.

Frieze A band of
horizontal carved
or painted
decoration or a
horizontal band of
wood – may run

along the top of a
bookcase under the
cornice or beneath
the top of a table.

Gadroon A
decorative border
formed from a
series of convex
flutes and curves.

Gesso Plaster-like
substance used as
a preparation in
gilded furniture.

Gilding Decorative
finish made by
covering a wooden
base with a layer
of gold leaf or
powdered gold.

Girandole A type
of elaborate
candelabrum or
a sconce with a
mirror behind,
made to hang on
the wall.

Greek key design
A geometric
decorative motif
taken from Ancient
Greek architecture.

Guéridon A small
French table,
usually in the form
of a column or
pedestal with a tray
top, to hold a
candlestick.

Guilloche
Decorative motif
inspired by Classical
antiquity, formed
from a continuous
figure-of-eight
pattern.

Hairy paw foot
Foot carved to
resemble a furry paw.

Harlequin Chairs of
similar design but
not a proper set; a
piece of furniture
with a mechanism
that when activated
pops open to reveal
hidden fittings.

Highboy American
term for a chest-
on-stand.

Inlay A design most
commonly cut
from veneers,
metal or mother-
of-pearl and set
into the surface of
a piece of furniture
to decorate it.

Intaglio A pattern
that is incised into
the surface.

Japanning
A European version
of Oriental lacquer
decoration.

Joined Furniture
constructed using
mortise and tenon
joints secured by
dowels.

Ladder-back Chair
with a back formed
from several
horizontal rails.

Lion's paw foot
Foot carved to
resemble a lion's
paw, a popular
form for early
19th-century
casters.

Loper A pull-out
support to hold up
the fall front of
a bureau.

Lunette Semi-
circular decorative

motif popular for carved friezes in the Jacobean and Victorian periods.

Marquetry A refined form of inlay using veneers of variously coloured woods to decorate a surface.

Nest of tables Set of graduated occasional tables that stack under each other when not in use.

Ogee Shallow double S-shape curve.

Ormolu Gilded bronze used for decorative mounts.

Parcel gilt Term used to describe a piece of furniture that is partially gilded.

Parquetry Geometric pattern used to decorate the surface of furniture, made from veneers of differently coloured woods.

Patina The accumulation of wax, polish and dirt that gives old furniture a characteristic soft appearance.

Pie-crust top Frilly carved decorative edge commonly seen on dish-top tripod tables.

Pier table Small side table made to stand

against the 'pier': the wall between two windows.

Pietre dure Inlay used to decorate furniture, made from thin slivers of hard and semi-precious stones.

Plinth A solid base.

Quarter-veneering A top veneered from four matching pieces of veneer.

Quartetto tables A graduated set of four small tables that nest together.

Reeding Fine parallel convex fluting used as a decorative motif on chair and table legs.

Re-entrant corner A corner that has been cut away with a decorative indentation, usually seen on the corners of table tops c.1720–1740.

Sabre leg Outward-curving tapered leg, typical of Regency chairs.

Seat rail Framework that supports the seat of a chair and holds the legs together.

Secretaire A writing cabinet with a flat front and a deep drawer that is hinged to open and form a writing surface.

Serpentine Undulating shallow double S-shape; this is the form often used on the fronts of quality furniture.

Settle An early form of bench with a back that could seat two or more people.

Shoe piece Piece of wood at the back of a chair that joins the base of the splat to the seat.

Spandrel Space between a corner and a central arch, often filled with decoration.

Splat Central flat piece of wood in a chair back.

Stretchers Horizontal bars joining and strengthening legs.

Stringing Fine inlaid lines around a piece of furniture, which were very popular in the Edwardian era.

Swan-neck handle A handle with sinuous curves at either end that was popular in the mid-18th century.

Teapoy Small container for holding and mixing tea, often resembling a casket on a pedestal stand.

Top-rail The highest horizontal bar on the back of a chair.

Trefoil Three-lobed Gothic decorative motif – like a stylized clover leaf.

Tripod table Popular small table with a tray top supported by a central pillar on a three-legged base.

Uprights The vertical pillars of a chair back.

Veneer Thin slices of wood used as a top, visible layer to decorate less expensive wood.

Whatnot A stand with open shelves for displaying small articles.

Windsor chair Provincial chair with solid seat and spindle back.

WHAT TO READ

**Magazines
& periodicals**
The Antique Collector
Magazine
The Antique Dealer
and Collectors'
Guide
The Art Newspaper
Homes & Antiques
The Antiques Trade
Gazette
House and Garden
World of Interiors

General books
Bly, John, *Is it
Genuine?* (1986)
Fleming, John, and
Honour, Hugh,
*The Penguin
Dictionary of the
Decorative Arts*
(1977)
Forrest, Tim, and
Kirkwood, John,
*Bonhams Directory:
Guide to Repairers
and Restorers*
(1994)
Hughes, Therle,
*The Country Life
Antiques Handbook*
(1986)
Miller, Martin
and Judith,
*Miller's Antiques
Price Guide* (1998)
*Miller's Antiques &
Collectables: The
Facts At Your
Fingertips* (1993)
*Miller's Understanding
Antiques* (1997)
Osborne, Harold,
*The Oxford
Companion to the
Decorative Arts*
(1985)

Simpson, M., and
Huntley, M. (Ed.)
*Sotheby's Caring for
Antiques* (1992)

Furniture books
Aguis, Pauline,
*British Furniture
1880–1915*
(1978)
Aslin, Elizabeth,
*Nineteenth Century
English Furniture*
(1962)
Bazin, Germain,
Baroque & Rococo
(1964)
Beard, Geoffrey, and
Gilbert,
Christopher (Ed.),
*Dictionary of English
Furniture-Makers*
(1968)
Bennett Oates,
Phyllis, *The Story of
Western Furniture*
(1981)
Bethnal Green
Museum, *Bentwood
Furniture: The Work
of Michael Thonet*
(1968)
Bly, John, *Discovering
English Furniture*
(1976)
Chinnery, Victor,
*Oak: The British
Tradition* (1979)
Coleridge, A.,
*Chippendale
Furniture* (1968)
Collard, Frances,
Regency Furniture
(1983)
Cooper, Jeremy,
*Victorian &
Edwardian Furniture*
(1987)

Edwards, Ralph,
*Shorter Dictionary of
English Furniture*
(1964)
Edwards, R., and
Jourdain, M.,
*Georgian Cabinet-
Makers* (1955)
Eriksen, Svend
*Early Neo-
classicism in France*
(1974)
Garner, Philippe,
*Twentieth Century
Furniture* (1980)
Grandjean, Serge,
Empire Furniture
(1966)
Hayward, Helena,
World Furniture
(1965)
Honour, Hugh,
*Cabinet-makers and
Furniture Designers*
(1969)
Jackson-Stops, G.,
and Pipkin, J.,
*The English Country
House* (1985)
Jervis, Simon,
Victorian Furniture
(1968)
Jourdain, Margaret,
Regency Furniture
(1965)
Joy, Edward T.,
*English Furniture
1800–1851*
(1977)
*Miller's Furniture:
Antiques Checklist*
(Davidson, R.,
consultant)
(1991)
*Miller's Late Georgian
to Edwardian
Furniture: Buyer's
Guide* (1998)

*Miller's Pine &
Country Furniture:
Buyer's Guide*
(1995)
Musgrave, Clifford,
*Adam, Hepplewhite
and other Neo-
classical Furniture*
(1966)
Ostergard, E. E.,
*Bentwood and Metal
Furniture 1850–
1980* (1987)
Payne, Christopher,
*Nineteenth
Century European
Furniture* (1996);
(Ed.) *Sotheby's
Concise
Encyclopedia of
Furniture* (1997)
Pevsner, Nicholas,
*Pioneers of Modern
Design* (1964)
Ward-Jackson, Peter,
*English Furniture
Design of the
Eighteenth
Century* (1958)
Wills, Geoffrey,
*English Furniture
1550–1760,*
(1971);
*English Furniture
1760–1900* (1971)
Wolsey, S. W., and
Luff, R.W. P.,
*Furniture in
England: The Age of
the Joiner* (1968)

INDEX

ACKNOWLEDGMENTS

The publishers would like to thank the following sources for supplying pictures for use in this book.

Front jacket tlSSx, trSL, brRB, blSL, cSL; **front flap** RB; **back jacket** SL; **back flap** SSx; 2tRB, tcRB, trSL, clSL, crSL, blRB, bcRB, brRB; 3tlSL, tcSL, trRB, blSL, bcRB, brRB; 10RB; 11SL; 12RB; 13SL; 14RB; 16RBx2; 17RB; 19RB; 20RBx2; 21P; 22P; 23P; 24RB; 25RB; 26RB; 27RB; 28RB; 29B; 31SL; 33RB; 34RB; 35RB; 36SL; 37RB; 38lRB, clCNY, crRB, rSL; 39RB; 40tlSSx, blRB, clSL, crRB, rRB; 41tlRB, tclRB, bclSL, tcrSL, bcrSL, rSL; 42RBx2; 43RBx3; 44lRB, cRB, rSL; 45RBx2; 46tlSL, clSL, crSL, rSL; 47SLx3; 48SLx3; 49SL; 50SL; 51SL; 52SSx; 53tSSx, cSSx, bRB; 54SSxx2; 55SLx2; 56tSL, bRB; 57RBx5; 58tRB, cSL, bRB; 59tlRB, trRB, bWillis Henry; 60lSL, rSSx; 61RB; 62SL; 63SLx3; 64SL; 65RB;

66ISL, cRB, rRB; 67lRB, cSL, rRB; 68tSL, rSSx, lSSx; 69SL; 72tRB, bSL; 73tRB, blSL, brSL; 74tSL, bSL; 75tRB, 75bSL; 76trRB, cSL, bSL; 77tlRB, trSL, cRB, brRB; 78SSx; 79tSL, cSL, bSL; 80SLx2; 81tSL, bRB; 82tRB, blRB, brRB; 83tSL, crRB, clRB, bRB; 85SSxx3; 86tSSx, bRB; 87tSL, bRB; 88tSL, bRB; 89SLx2; 90tSL, bSL; 91tSL, cSL, bP; 94tSL, bSL; 95tSL, cSL, bSL; 96SLx2, bRB; 97lSL, rRBx2; 98RBx3; 99tRB, cSL, bRB; 100lRB, rRB; 101lRB, rSL; 102lRB, cSL, rRB; 103ISL, cRB, rRB; 104SL; 105tlRB, crSL, blRB, brRB; 106SSxx3; 107SSx; 108SL, trRB, blSL; 109RB; 110trSSx, bSL; 111trSSx, cRB; brRB; 112rSL, ISL; 113tSSx, cSSx, bRB; 114tSL, brSL, blRB; 115tlRB, trSL, blSL, brSL; 116SSx; 117SSxx2; 118SSxx2; 119SSx; 120tSL, bSL; 121tSL, cSL, bSL; 122RBx2; 123SLx2; 124tSL, bSL; 125tSL, cSL, bSL; 126SSx; 127tSL; cSL, bRB;

128tSL; blSL; brRB; 129SL; 130trSL; cSL; brSSx; 131tSL; cRB; brRB; 132SLx2; 133SLx2; 134lSL, rSL; 135tSL, cSL, bSL; 136SSx; 137tSL, bSL; 138tSL, bSL; 139tSL, cSL, bSL; 140lSL, rSL; 141tSL, lSL, bRB; 142tSL, bRB; 143tSL, clSL, clSL; 144tRB, bRBx2; 145tSL, clRB, crRB, bRB; 146SSxx2, 147tD, cSSx, blSSx; 148lSSx; 149tRB, cRB, blRB, brRB; 150tlRB, trRB, bRB; 151Lloyd Loom, cRB; 152lSSx, bSL; 153RBx2; 154lRB/SL, rSSx, bRB; 155tRB, cRBx2, bSSx; 156RBx2; 157RBx3; 158RBx3; 159RBx2; 160tSL, blSL, brSRB; 16tlSL, cSL, rSL; 162RBx4; 163tlSL, trRB, cSSx, bSL; 164tRB, rSL, lRB; 165tSL, cSL, bSL; 166tRB, cRB, bSL; 167tRB, tlRB, cRB, bSL; 168tSL, cSL, bSL; 169tSSx, clSL, crSL, bSL; 170tRB, cRB, bRB; 171tSL, cSL, bRB; 172RB; 173tRB, cRB, bB; 174Bx2; 175tB, cB, blRB, brRB; 176RB.

Key

t top; c centre; b bottom; l left; r right; **B** Bonhams; **D** Drummonds of Bramley, Kent; **P** Penman Antiques Fairs; **RB** Reed Consumer Books; **SL** Sotheby's London; **SSx** Sotheby's Sussex.

Special photography on pp.10, 16, 17, 18, 25 by Jacqui Hurst on behalf of Reed Consumer Books.

Special photography on pp.2, 3, 14, 17, 19, 20, 24, 25, 27, 28, 33, 34, 35, 37, 38, 40, 41, 42, 43, 44, 45, 53, 56, 57, 58, 61, 65, 66, 67, 72, 73, 75, 76, 77, 81, 82, 83, 86, 87, 88, 97, 98, 99, 100, 101, 102, 103, 109, 110, 112, 113, 114, 115, 122, 127, 128, 131, 141, 142, 144, 145, 149, 150, 151, 153, 154, 155, 156, 157, 158, 159, 160, 162, 164, 166, 167, 170, 171, 172, 175, 176 by Ian Booth on behalf of Reed Consumer Books.

Special photograaphy on pp.12, 26 by James Merrell on behalf of Reed Consumer Books.

The author would like to thank Alex Payne of Bonhams for his invaluable assistance in compiling the section on 20th-century designers, Maxine Fox, Samantha Georgeson and Elin Jones of Sotheby's for their help with researching photographs and Henry House of Christie's for his help with updating the text.

The publishers would like to thank the following individuals and companies for allowing their items to be photographed: Sotheby's in London, Phoenix Hire in London, William Clegg at The Country Seat, Nr Henley in Oxon, Country Pine Antiques, Rochester in Kent and The Pine Mine in London.